lieves Giraudoux can interpret Electra
as one who wills to live and does so
without violence to his model and with
expression of a prevalent modern theme.
Oedipus, on the other hand, one of the
most powerful of Sophocles' figures, is
too completely realized and too entirely
defined by prophesy and by his insistence upon truth to allow for meaningful
reinterpretation.

This provocative thesis will in-
trigue all who share an interest in
drama—classical or modern.

ABOUT THE AUTHOR

Käte Hamburger is Professor of General and Comparative Literature at the
Technical Institute of Stuttgart and has
published several books of criticism including a study of Thomas Mann. Literature is her subject of study, but her
degree, taken after study in Berlin and
Munich, was in philosophy. During
World War II she lived in France and
Sweden.

FROM SOPHOCLES TO SARTRE

FROM SOPHOCLES TO SARTRE

Figures from Greek Tragedy,
Classical and Modern

KÄTE HAMBURGER

Translated by Helen Sebba

FREDERICK UNGAR PUBLISHING CO. New York

Translated from the German *Von Sophokles zu Sartre:*
Griechische Dramenfiguren antik und modern, © 1962, by arrangement
with Verlag W. Kohlhammer GmbH. Stuttgart

But millennia are living in our minds, lost things, unspoken things, dust;
Cain and Zenobia. The Atridae flourish the thyrsus.

GOTTFRIED BENN
Roman des Phänotyp

FOREWORD

This little book grew out of a course of lectures given at the Stuttgart Technische Hochschule in response to the interest which the numerous contemporary adaptations of Greek tragedies were then arousing. I never intended to publish them, and only the kind interest of the publishers, who suggested the title, and of a number of people who heard the lectures have persuaded me to let them appear, revised and expanded, in book form. The book's claim is still no more than that of the original lectures : to satisfy a potential current interest in this subject.

K. H.

Stuttgart
March 1962

CONTENTS

INTRODUCTION

As I said in my foreword, the subject of this book was suggested by the numerous adaptations of Greek tragic themes that have enriched world drama in recent decades, some of which, like Sartre's *The Flies*, Giraudoux's *Electra*, and Anouilh's *Antigone*, have played a significant part in shaping its profile. At this time I merely want to state this fact, without drawing any speculative conclusions as to a particular affinity between our times and Greek antiquity. This reworking of Greek themes, present throughout the history of Western ideas, has its origin in the formative role played by Greek philosophy, literature, and art in the establishment of our culture and more specifically in the artistic—that is, plastic—creative genius of "antiquity." The Greek spirit is the figure-creating spirit, as Greek sculpture and literature testify, as do philosophic concepts such as Plato's doctrine of ideas, the doctrine of spiritual entities as figures (however immaterially conceived) placed "beyond the heavens." But alongside Greek sculpture in its golden age stands Greek drama, the plastic, figure-creating genre of literature; alongside Phidias stand Aeschylus, Sophocles, and Euripides.

In this context we may disregard the *form* of Greek tragedy. For the ferment which the Greek plays introduced into dramatic literature and which is still at work today, perpetually creating and re-creating, did not stem from its distinctive dramatic form, determined by the chorus and by stichomythic dialogue, but from its characters. The chorus disappeared in the modern era and was

1

reinstated only when some writer deliberately sought to renew the Greek dramatic form, as Schiller did in *The Bride of Messina* or as T. S. Eliot did in a different way in *Murder in the Cathedral*. But Orestes, Electra and Iphigenia, Oedipus and Antigone, Phaedra, Medea, and Alcestis are figures which remain forever alive, constantly being shaped and reshaped by the various dramatic and linguistic styles of succeeding centuries—and by no means only in periods of classical revival such as Latin humanism, French classicism, and the German classical age. As for contemporary versions of Greek tragic figures, they are no more "modern" compared to their models than were Racine's Phaedra, Goethe's Iphigenia, or Grillparzer's Medea compared to their originals in Euripides.

In fact, we fully appreciate the miracle of the prototypal Greek figures only when we recognize their constant modernity in all the diverse periods and contexts of their dramatic reincarnations. We are compelled to ask what the concept "figure" can actually mean. Aristotle maintained in his *Poetics* that the essential thing in tragedy was not the characters but the events, the fable, the *mythos,* and the action compounded from it. For him the preeminent example, which he repeatedly cites as a model tragedy, was Sophocles' *Oedipus,* in which the action, the "destiny," takes precedence over character. This may not seem completely applicable to dramatic figures such as Sophocles' Electra and Antigone, Euripides' Medea, or even the Clytemnestra of Aeschylus' *Oresteia,* since they obviously present very pronounced character traits as well as actions and decisions deriving from individual will; yet even so we must bear Aristotle's statement in mind.

Another passage in the *Poetics* will help us to comprehend this statement in a larger sense. A poet, it says, should depict not what has happened but what might have happened according to probability and necessity. What distinguishes the poet from the historian is that the poet describes "the universal," and the historian, the special case. The traditional—and not immediately transparent —text goes on to explain that history tells us what, say, an Alcibiades did or had done to him, whereas the statements of poetry "are of the nature rather of universals, . . . [statements] as to what such or such a kind of man will probably or necessarily say or do" (1451b). To elucidate : unlike the historian, who is concerned solely with facts, the poet does indeed need characters—and specific characters; nevertheless the theme of poetry is not the portrayal of characters as such. They represent just one element in the dramatic action, which consists in creating a plausible situation in which a certain man, having certain character traits, speaks and acts in a certain way. Unlike the historian, the poet is not obliged to stick to the given facts of each particular case. He can construct or invent facts; out of people and circumstances he can develop situations which will produce a particular effect upon the audience, namely, pity and fear. And the specifically tragic situations that he creates do exactly this. Aristotle defines them in the widest sense as situations in which a man is stricken by misfortune, and the way this first analyst of tragedy conceives and outlines such situations is illuminating for our investigation into the constant potential "modernity" of the themes and characters of Greek drama.

It is not tragic, says Aristotle, when a thoroughly bad man or a thoroughly good man falls into misfortune. Neither case produces the indispensable effect of tragedy : the arousing of pity and fear. In the case of the good man, the misfortune is merely shocking. A situation is felt to be tragic—that is, it inspires pity and fear only when it involves a man who is not outstanding in virtue and whose misfortune stems not from his own turpitude but from a mistaken act (hamaartia). Rules of this sort, especially the case of the good man overcome by misfortune, seem odd to us. At first glance it is quite incomprehensible why the misfortune of a thoroughly good man should be less tragic, less worthy of pity, than that of a normal, average man, whose tragedy stems purely from his having made a mistake. Closer examination shows that these rules are connected with the situation theory or plot theory of Aristotelian dramaturgy. Attention is not to be directed to the characters as such, as would inevitably happen if thoroughly good or thoroughly bad men were depicted. The essential thing is the tragic effect itself, which is achieved not through particularly outstanding characters but through the situation—specifically the kind of situation in which any normal man may find himself.

Aristotle's situation theory is further illuminated by a requirement which he merely suggests and which is discussed in detail only by the later classicistic poets Corneille and Lessing : the requirement of fear (or terror) as the emotion aroused in a spectator by the fate of a man "like himself" (1453a). Aristotle recognizes as the theme of tragedy a man being cast into a painful situation in which he behaves "in one way or another." Orestes in the situation of having to kill his mother; Electra in the situation of having to live in the house of her mother, her father's murderess; Oedipus confronted with the discovery that he has killed his father and married his mother; Antigone forced to bury her brother in defiance of the king's decree; Phaedra overwhelmed by unrequited love for her stepson; Medea abandoned by her husband—these are for Aristotle the subjects of Greek tragedy. From them he derives his theory of tragedy as the representation of people in action, which for him means people behaving in one way or another in the tragic situation.

We have said that the characters of Greek tragedy, not its artistic form, are perpetually capable of becoming "modern" and of challenging dramatists to reinterpret them. It must in fact be stressed—and this is supported by Aristotle's analysis—that this concept of the figure is not realized through characters of one particular bent or another but purely through the situations created by the tragedians in which men find themselves and in which they behave "in one way or another." This is the origin of the consistency as well as the variability that has given rise to reinterpretations of these figures. In fact, the tragedians themselves reshaped them : Sophocles created a different Electra from Aeschylus, and Euripides a different one from Sophocles, to mention just three of the surviving examples of classical versions. Consistency of theme, and hence of situation, and variability in the characters' behavior may be called the basic schema responsible for the persistent creative impetus that emanates from the figures of Greek drama.

But this still does not definitively explain the ultimate reason for this impetus. Although Aristotle associates the spectator's sympathy with his being able to recognize the individuals on whom tragedy befalls as like himself, the situations are in most cases so extreme, so far outside normal circumstances, that the constant challenge to create new versions—a challenge that these plays have offered dramatists right down to our own time—seems startling. Thus Corneille found it remarkable that Aristotle should expect the spectator to regard a figure such as Oedipus as a man like himself, since he could hardly imagine himself in the extremely anomalous position of Oedipus.[1] Human sacrifice, the murder of a husband or wife, matricide, infanticide, men led astray by oracles, blood feuds, and divine decree—all these exigencies and situations seem so bound up with archaic times, so inapplicable to other ages, that the challenge to use them as themes again and again, to "modernize" them, is an astounding phenomenon. It is a different phenomenon, a different process, from purely historical interest in the antique works themselves. A contemporary staging of Sophocles' *Antigone* is one thing; the existence of Anouilh's *Antigone* is another. Interest in classical drama for its own sake is no different from interest in the drama of any other era of the past, in Shakespeare, say, or Corneille or Schiller. The distinctive, unique phenomenon is the fact that the themes and characters of Greek drama are the only ones to have survived as a perpetual creative force. Where should we seek the explanation—or, to be more cautious—*an* explanation for this?

Let us examine once again the concept of the situation. We said that although the situation remains constant throughout the various versions, it nevertheless constitutes the real germ of the reinterpretations: the situation of Orestes forced to commit matricide, of Antigone forced to bury her brother in defiance of the king's decree. It is clear that we must interpret these situations in a wider sense and that the tragedians themselves open the way for this. For behind the pros and cons surrounding the enactment of these singular deeds, they themselves already raise the question of the *possibilities* of human will, human imperatives, human capacities, the question of justice and injustice, freedom and non-freedom, the absoluteness and the limitations of human existence. This is perhaps the ultimate explanation of the persistent stimulus that emanates from Attic tragedy : here *for the first time* poetry was depicting human existential problems, and precisely for this reason the events, the external situations through which it presented them, have remained exemplary. For the very changes in these existential problems became visible by contrast with the unchanging nature of the situation in the classical plays and the various modern versions.

The broader horizons of our theme warrant some further examination of this significant aspect of Attic tragedy : its unprecedentedness; for this is precisely what gives it its prototypal, elemental quality and hence its forcefulness as a model.

It begins with something which at first glance may appear trivial, unconnected with any world view, a purely formal matter : the dialogic structure of this poetic genre. When a *choreut* turned to face the chorus as it danced and sang its dithyrambs in honor of Dionysus, and thus became the *hypokrites*, the answerer, dialogue form was born, out of which Greek tragedy—or, more generally, drama—grew. Aeschylus later developed the form further by introducing two actors; Sophocles added a third, and there it stopped. (This does not mean that the number of characters was limited to the number of actors, but merely that no more than three people in addition to the chorus were ever on stage together.)

The essential thing about the creation of the dramatic form through the addition of one single actor is that it produced a richer dialogue, in which the chorus too played a more active role. The chorus itself becomes an answerer and thus takes on the character of specific groups which are related, closely or more distantly, to the active personages : the elders or the women of a city, maid-servants, and so on. It always represents a cohesive body and expresses itself in the first person singular. But the very fact that a body, a group of people, appears on stage as one single person, that is to say, confronts another person as a speaker, demonstrates the significance and function of the dialogue structure. This structure is modified still further when the chorus divides into two people talking to one another : chorus and chorus leader.

These are well-known facts, briefly sketched and recalled as a preliminary to the question that interests us : what this dialogue form, which is the essence of drama, indicates. In this connection, only its emergence, its first appearance, is revealing—not the form itself, which was established once and for all to survive through centuries of linguistic and formal variations because of the indissoluble link between the drama and the theatre : the indispensable self-portrayal of the characters. The only thing that concerns us here is what the dialogue-based dramatic form reveals in its relation to the narrative form of the Homeric epic, not to narrative poetry of later eras, especially more recent or modern ones. For those later works no longer present the complex of plot and meaning which forms the contrasting background to the Attic drama. This gives it —and indeed the dramatic form of poetry as such—its historical significance, for here, by contrast to the epic, man's emerging awareness of himself finds its poetic expression. This still leaves out of consideration the general evolution of the Greek spirit as expressed in philosophy, art, and politics. We have confined ourselves strictly to what is indicated by the *forms* of narrative and dramatic poetry—and it was no accident that the rise of tragedy coincided three-hundred years later with the flowering of philosophy and art in the age of Pericles.

Not by chance did epic poetry exist long before dramatic poetry, in Greece and everywhere else. Narrative was then and is now the spontaneous form; what comes first is the account of events, and of people only insofar as they are the vehicles of events. The *Iliad* does not recount the episodes of the Trojan War for the sake of the people who figure in them. Homer does not tell his stories for the sake of describing and characterizing Achilles, Agamemnon, Menelaus, Hector, Patroclus, or Helen, or just to tell what happened to them, but in order to recount that episode in the war which was caused by the anger of Achilles. This is not to say that these figures did not emerge as individuals, traditionally endowed with certain characteristics. We have only to hear their names to know what they are. But what they are is identical with what they do, with their function in the occurrence of events.

At this point in the war Achilles is the man of anger. His anger is the essential thing; this is what the muse must sing. Agamemnon is the mightiest prince in Greece, the leader of the Achaeans. He refuses to relinquish his slave Briseis to Achilles, who sulks and refuses to fight. But neither Agamemnon's pettiness nor Achilles' obstinacy and readiness to let a personal grudge override the interests of their cause is ever discussed in the Homeric epic or made the occasion for censuring these heroes. "To be sure," said Hegel, "so far as Achilles' anger is concerned, we may well moralize about the harm and destruction it caused and draw a disparaging conclusion about the preeminence and greatness of Achilles himself. . . .But Achilles is not to be censured, and we have no need to excuse his anger just because of his other great qualities. Achilles is simply the man he is, and from the epic standpoint that is that."[2] The fact that Helen's adultery with Paris causes the war and the death of so many heroes is not made a subject for moralizing; only her beauty emerges as a matter of fact. Helen's beauty, her abduction to Troy, Achilles' anger, and Agamemnon's resentment are facts, just like the events of the war. The characters exist and are described for the sake of the events, not vice versa. The aim of Homer's epic poetry is to describe a tremendous world upheaval.

The characters are caught in the flood of events, and the question of their attitude to those events is never raised. Man as such has not yet become a problem.

This is true even when the psychological condition of these marvelously realistic characters is described : Andromache taking leave of Hector, with all her fears and anxieties for her husband, her heartrending lament after he has been killed, or Achilles in his boundless grief for Patroclus throwing himself upon his couch, weeping and sleepless. The suffering which war inflicts upon men is graphically depicted in these scenes of grief and pain, but exactly the same graphic realism differentiates the portraits of the warrior heroes. The one portrays life just as the other does. Events roll on; the war rolls on. Andromache's scene is just one scene from life among others. The narrative overtakes her and leaves her behind again, as life in its ever-changing aspects and situations overtakes men and their joys and sorrows. The characters are the vehicles of the events, caught up and swept along in their current. The listener can no more dwell upon them than can the rhapsodist who recounts them. The primal narrative situation, the storytelling rhapsodist and his listening audience, is the prerequisite for the original epic portrayal of man and the world.

Against the background of the Homeric epic we see what the drama signifies three centuries later. We see this from its dialogue form. The form itself makes a statement, expresses the fact that the relationship between personage and event has been reversed. When the characters portray themselves, speaking without a narrator as intermediary, and can thus appear on stage concretely and tangibly impersonated by the actor, then a shift of interest and perspective occurs involuntarily, as it were. The spectator encounters people to whom something happens—and only such people.

When the Trojan War becomes the theme, notably in Euripides' *Trojan Women, Hecuba, Helen,* and *Andromache,* it is no longer merely the currently dominant condition of life, of which suffering and misfortune are a part, just like battles, defeat, and victory. The war now becomes a problem, a subject of lament and protest. Attempts are made to find what man or god is responsible for the misfortune that has overwhelmed Ilium and the Trojan women. Man begins to resist, and Euripides' Andromache, now the captive of Pyrrhus, says :

These same lamentations
Sobbings and tears to which my days are given
I'll now storm heaven with. For nature tempers
The souls of women so they find a pleasure
In voicing their afflictions as they come.[3]

It is easy to recognize how significant for the depiction of man these figures are who speak for themselves and reveal themselves. Even when they are speaking about the events which befall them, they are making statements about themselves. Their actions and reactions are not spontaneous happenings but seem to be caused by their thoughts, their emotions, even if it is only in resisting fate, as in the case of the Trojan women, or yielding to it. Now we are interested not only in what happens but in how people deal with the events and react to them. Homer never raises the question of the guilt and responsibility of Paris and Helen; Helen's abduction is the cause of the war as some other event might have been and is accepted as such. Euripides raises the question; his plays portray and discuss her personality in ever-new variations. If we were to imagine the extreme coincidences through which Oedipus becomes the murderer of his father and the husband of his mother as Homer would have narrated them, they would seem like the involved plot of a mystery novel. Not through the events alone did Sophocles' Oedipus establish himself ineradicably in the human consciousness, but through the figure of the king, fatally entangled in guilt and suffering, who puts out his own eyes, through the problem which his fate makes visible in its most extreme form: how man can incur guilt without his own knowledge or will.

Yet to mention one of these Sophoclean characters even as an illustration makes the mere structural basis of the drama from which we started out, namely dialogue, seem irrelevant in comparison with the figure created here, or, speaking in terms of form, in comparison with the sophisticated analytical technique which makes this tragedy so powerful. The same applies to all the works of the tragedians, in fact to Greek tragedy as a whole, as it stands forth like a model at the beginning of Western drama. We have called attention to the formal germ, the structural element, from which this flowering of dramatic art stemmed, because this and not the Homeric epic first opened the way for the portrayal of man.

It is impossible to say whether or to what extent the evolution

of the Greek spirit, with its urge to depict human existential problems, caused or fecundated the formal emergence of the drama.
Even if we accept the proposition that the singling out of the
answerer from the Dionysian chorus marks the origin of the
dramatic genre, nevertheless tragedy itself, as the expression of a
more advanced intellectual level, is not yet discernible in this formal
event. The question can only be posed, not definitely answered,
whether and where the two processes are genetically and historically
connected. From the standpoint of the theory of literature and
literary genres, the miracle of Greek tragedy is enhanced rather
than diminished by an appreciation of what the dialogue form as
opposed to the narrative form meant for the depiction of human
problems.

The formal difference between Attic drama and the Homeric
epic demonstrates with a clarity and simplicity never again possible
the formative influence of Greek tragedy not upon Western drama
alone, but upon the whole view of man. For later, after narrative
writing had abandoned its original epic, Homeric mode in favor of
the modern novelistic form, the primacy of event over character
became blurred and disappeared; that is, the problem of man in its
widest sense becomes the theme of narrative no less than dramatic
writing.

Goethe still had the Homeric epic in mind when, in his cor-
respondence with Schiller in December, 1797, he associated tragedy
with the depiction of "man turned inward" in contrast to the epic
poem, which he said represented "man in action outside himself."
Goethe (who by then had already written *Wilhelm Meister*) did not
include the novel in these associations; in fact he barely recognized
it as epic writing. But the very existence of the novel makes this
distinction invalid long before Goethe's time, for it was no longer
true that only tragedy depicted "man turned inward." It was not
even applicable to the courtly verse epic, despite its broad-scale
description of events and of the world (still the epic substance of
the novel) or of a love novel such as Gottfried's *Tristan und Isolde*,
to mention just one particularly striking example. In the era of the
novel, problems of "man turned inward," human existential situations, became and still are thematic for both genres, and it is
symptomatic of this connection that the concept of the Tragic
originally derived from tragedy could no longer be restricted to the
drama.

However, the concept of the Tragic as Aristotle defined it for Greek tragedy did distinguish Greek tragedy from Homeric epic. And if we take this concept—as Aristotle's definition allows—as a designation of existential situations in general, then in this existentially intended filling out or interpretation of the somewhat empty word "tragedy" (which meant nothing more than "goat song"), Aristotle, the great phenomenologist, identified the formative significance of the Attic drama in conceiving and portraying man and his situation. Yet this first interpreter of the first dramatic literature would not have recognized this significance if the drama had not demonstrated it in such an exemplary manner. And this is what, even today, still strikes us as the miracle of Greek tragedy. Of course it demonstrated its significance through the artistic perfection of its form. But breaking out of this historical form, so to speak, it lives on in the transformations of its figures at the hand of later ages—eternal figures which are eternal precisely because they became symbols of fundamental situations. The fact that these situations were presented in infinite variations, with major or minor changes—so that Sartre's Orestes, for instance, seems to have nothing in common with the Orestes of Aeschylus, and Goethe's Iphigenia nothing in common with Euripides'—is but one side of the dialectical relationship existing here : that Sartre's Orestes is still an Orestes and Anouilh's Antigone still an Antigone. The constancy of the figures within the variations of the thematic problem is just a sign of the immutability of the fundamental situations established by the tragedians.[4]

The viewpoint of our comparative interpretation has now been stated. It consists in the simple idea that it is no accident that the figures of Greek tragedy survived as a creative stimulus in the drama of later eras. This idea has determined the main line of the present study, which diverges a little from earlier methods of examining Greek dramatic themes. Those approaches—an academic example of which is the standard essay topic "Compare Goethe's *Iphigenia* with the *Iphigenia* of Euripides"—have been primarily interested in the reshaping of classical models by modern writers. Otherwise, the interpretation of such dramas, particularly in our own time, usually confines itself to its own sphere, examining them —quite justifiably—in relation to the other works of the author in question. This method is no doubt dictated by the wide, often extreme, divergence of the modern works from the classical ones (especially French works like those of Sartre, Giraudoux, and Anouilh, which are also modern in form), which seems to preclude comparison.

Our purpose, by contrast, is not merely to recognize the re-interpretation as such but to investigate the germ, often hidden, in the Greek model, that may have produced the modern version. This procedure proves especially illuminating for contemporary versions because our own time, while having fewer scholarly links with antiquity than the eighteenth and nineteenth centuries, has been able, through the broadening of its knowledge and perspective in other fields such as psychology, mythology, and archaeology, to discover much in the Greek classics that was not accessible to earlier eras, especially the humanistic ones.

Thus our method aims at understanding the Greek figures in their classical as well as their modern being and meaning. This implies that we shall make connections as well as distinctions and differentiations and shall neither interpret modern works in an archaic way nor—as would be more dangerous—interpret Greek antiquity in a modern way. The theme is a duration within change, having its ultimate basis in that duration within change that stamps human history as the history of human beings.

A few more observations on the treatment of this theme may be added. Although, as we said at the outset, this comparative study focuses upon the relationship of Greek plays of our time, or at least of our century, to their Greek models, works of other periods will be discussed whenever this seems useful and illuminating in profiling the thematic problems. Goethe's Iphigenia, for example, stands so meaningfully between Euripides and Gerhart Hauptmann, or Grillparzer's Medea between Euripides and Anouilh, that the specific thematic problems of the modern versions emerge particu-larly clearly when the modern figures are matched against their counterparts from the idealistic age of German literature.

These additions are balanced by an omission—or what may look like an omission. Since we are concerned only with the concep-tion of the characters and the changes they have undergone, we have not been concerned with the structure of the plays or gone into the details of the action. In many cases, indeed, we have had to forgo a complete analysis which would categorize every motif and every figure in the individual classical and modern works, because this would have meant deviating from our comparative viewpoint. This study does not pretend to be New Criticism in the stricter sense, any more than it is a critical evaluation. Its theme thus stands slightly apart from the requirements of literary scholarship, particularly contemporary literary scholarship, which is more aware than ever before of style and technique and more interested in the process of creation than in the finished product. Perhaps the lack of modernity in method may be counterbalanced by the modernity of the subject matter : the continuing survival of the classical figures in our own dramatic literature. This also implies that we have not tried to treat the subject exhaustively or to give a chronological presentation of every version of the Greek plays from the tragedians through Seneca down to modern times.[5] Only those characters are discussed that are interesting—or that seem to us interesting—in connection with the various thematic problems.

In another respect, too, this study doubtless falls short of what its subject matter, tragedies of world literature, would demand : it undertakes no analysis of the problem of the Tragic itself. It seeks to present the material as directly as possible, to look at the characters themselves, and is no more concerned with their function as representatives of Tragedy than were, in our opinion, their creators, classical and modern. The point is this : the tragic situations are indeed the situations of the characters in the sense in which Aristotle defined the concept, the sense of a man's being cast into misfortune (and here we can ignore his rules about the thoroughly good or bad man). What is being presented and thus made visible is the *situation,* not the tragic element it contains. The concept, the particular nature and structure of the tragic element in each of the directly presented tragic situations, are themselves the product of abstract thought, indeed of a theory—and not one single theory either— whose material is the constantly differentiated "life" of the figures, their being and fate, their suffering and their problem. This little book seeks merely to interpret the phenomena which the behavior of Greek dramatic characters, classical and modern, provides for comparative study. It makes no claim to deduce from them any theory or any conceptual definitions of tragedy itself. And even so far as the interpretation of the phenomena goes, it is no more immune to relativity and subjectivity than is any attempt at interpretation.[6]

I

CLYTEMNESTRA

We begin with the tragedians' most powerful subject, the legend of the House of Atreus. The story of this accursed family begins with Atreus, who in his struggle for supremacy with his brother Thyestes committed the monstrous crime of killing all Thyestes' sons except Aegisthus, the youngest, and serving their flesh to their father at table. The curse which Atreus thus called down upon his house enigmatically pervades the history of his sons, Agamemnon and Menelaus, and their disastrous marriages to Leda's daughters, Clytemnestra and Helen, both adulteresses. Although Helen caused the Trojan War, bringing more misfortune upon the House of Atreus, she herself was immune to destruction because of her semi-divine birth as the daughter of Leda and Zeus (an immunity which also extended to her husband). However, Agamemnon, the proud and mighty prince and victorious leader of the Achaeans, is brought to ruin between the beginning of the war and its end. To induce Artemis to send favorable winds he is forced to sacrifice his eldest daughter, Iphigenia, at Aulis. Twenty years later Clytemnestra, now long married to Aegisthus, will cite Agamemnon's guilt toward Iphigenia in explanation of her murder of her returning husband, only to be killed herself in retribution by her son Orestes.

It is upon Agamemnon's house that the curse of the Atridae rests, and it is not surprising that this saga of destiny, lust, guilt, and bitter remorse should have attracted the dramatists. The three Greek tragedians all played their part in shaping the story. As the subject

15

of the *Oresteia* trilogy of Aeschylus, the first tragedian, the Atridae theme stands at the very beginning of Western drama, which this triology, the most powerful of Aeschylus' five extant works, may actually be said to have founded.

Looking more closely at the way the characters in this saga behave in the course of world drama from Aeschylus to O'Neill and Sartre, from Sophocles to Hofmannsthal and Giraudoux, from Euripides to Hauptmann, we are immediately struck by the fact that dramatic interest has focused chiefly on the children of Agamemnon and Clytemnestra, the last generation of the House of Atreus. The isolated single plays dealing exclusively with the story of the parents' marriage and consequently with Clytemnestra's relationship to Aegisthus are forced into the background by the profusion of plays about Orestes and Electra in world literature. Among them Seneca's *Agamemnon* and the *Agamemnon of* the Italian dramatist Vittorio Alfieri, written in 1786, may be mentioned simply as works of famous writers.

The position is different when the whole family history from the Trojan War on is presented in trilogies or tetralogies, first by Aeschylus, then not again until O'Neill (in a modern guise) and Gerhart Hauptmann. These works all include an Agamemnon play and hence a dramatization of Clytemnestra's adultery and murder of her husband. But in every case, in Aeschylus as well as in both the modern dramatists, the murder of the husband is incorporated, as a separate play, into the story of the final generation as the prehistory to the story of Orestes and Electra, or in Hauptmann—more essentially still—into the Iphigenia story. As we shall see, this is done differently in all three cases, depending on which aspect of the tragedy as a whole is to be accentuated. Except for the Seneca play and Alfieri's intrinsically more important one (to which we shall return), literature seems to have found the marital tragedy of Agamemnon and Clytemnestra insufficiently substantial to provide the theme for a separate full-scale treatment.

The reason for this may be a relative lack of psychological interest in the adultery story, but more likely it is the fact that the murder of the husband bore within it the murder of the mother. As a problem, Orestes' murder of his mother overshadows Clytemnestra's murder of her husband. So far as I know, only Alfieri has reversed this relationship; his Orestes play, which is a sequel to the

Agamemnon, is dominated by the problem of Clytemnestra. Elsewhere, however, dramatic interest did not center upon what led Clytemnestra to her action; her function is primarily to have committed it and to be shaped by it. Even when a motivation is suggested—usually revenge for the sacrifice of Iphigenia—the murder of the husband is still no more than the prehistory to the matricide. Above all, the matricide precipitates the problem of man forced into a situation, the problem of decision and action, while the murder of the husband is simply an event of sensual passion and thus less problematical, if not in itself, then at least in the legend as a whole, than the terrible deed of Clytemnestra's children against their mother. Only Orestes and Electra are truly thematic figures in European drama; Clytemnestra becomes thematic only in relation to them and Agamemnon, who is an active character in plays about Iphigenia, and Aegisthus both stand in Clytemnestra's magnetic field.

Because the theme of the *Oresteia* at every turn in its development is linked to Clytemnestra as the victim of Orestes' deed or as the object of Electra's hatred, Aeschylus made sure that she would go down in literature as a woman formed by her deed and taking full responsibility for it. As we have said, Aeschylus devoted the first play of the *Oresteia,* the *Agamemnon,* to establishing this. And it was by no means self-evident, because the epic tradition, as Homer recorded it in the third book of the *Odyssey,* says that Aegisthus committed the murder and Clytemnestra merely aided him. Once Clytemnestra becomes the principal perpetrator, however, the matricide achieves its full poignancy as the result of her having murdered her husband, and moreover her personality is established once and for all in the monumental contours of an imperious woman with a lust for power, ambiguous and ultimately inscrutable in her motives but from the outset unambiguous and purposeful in her actions.

After many years of marriage to Aegisthus she greets the returning Agamemnon with words of joy, bidding the herald :

> Tell this to my husband,
> To come with all speed, the city's darling;
> May he returning find a wife as loyal
> As when he left her, watchdog of the house.[1]

It is perfectly obvious—and the audience is perfectly aware—that she is speaking hypocritically. But how does Aeschylus bring this out within the play itself? This skillful writer does not abandon the rules of dramatic technique just because of his audience's knowledge of history. When Agamemnon and Clytemnestra have gone into the house and the chorus expresses its premonitions and fears, predicting the horror which threatens, Cassandra the seer, Priam's daughter, whom Agamemnon has brought with him as a prize of war and concubine, is left standing motionless on his chariot. Her function is to set the coming crime in its context, to expose Clytemnestra's hypocrisy immediately, leaving no doubt or uncertainty even within the play itself.

Inspired by Apollo, Cassandra shrieks her stark words of prophecy :

> Quick! Be on your guard! The bull—
> Keep him clear of the cow.
> Caught with a trick, the black horn's point,
> She strikes. He falls; lies in the water.
> Murder; a trick in a bath. I tell what I see.   (p. 63)

Because what is happening offstage is described simultaneously in a prophetic vision instead of being reported later by a messenger, the old familiar events acquire dramatic tension and the horror is made real. At the same time this marvelously effective device starkly spotlights the crux of this play : the murder of the husband and the murderer herself. The only decisive scene is the one where Clytemnestra in her terrible triumph comes out of the palace door with the murder weapon on her shoulder and without the least compunction renders her account :

> And with that he spits his life out where he lies
> And smartly spouting blood he sprays me with
> The sombre drizzle of bloody dew and I
> Rejoice no less than in God's gift of rain
> The crops are glad when the ear of corn gives birth.
> These things being so, you elders of Argos,
> Rejoice if rejoice you will. Mine is the glory.   (pp. 69–70)

It would certainly be too modern to speak of her ghastly triumph as cynicism; this powerful, demonic figure is not so intellectually conceived. What Aeschylus is expressing here is the unproblematic action of an unproblematic, instinctive nature. Yet it is not unproblematic in the sense that Clytemnestra does not try to justify herself in the eyes of the elders of the city. She recalls the sacrifice of Iphigenia, alludes to Agamemnon's love affair with Cassandra (though without drawing the parallel of her own adultery), and finally adduces the curse on the House of Atreus of which she claims to have been merely the instrument :

> You say this is my work—mine?
> Do not cozen yourself that I am Agamemnon's wife.
> Masquerading as the wife
> Of the corpse there the old sharp-witted Genius
> Of Atreus who gave the cruel banquet
> Has paid with a grown man's life
> The due for children dead.   (p. 72)

After some initial resistance, the chorus accepts her excuses, though hesitantly : "That you are not guilty of this murder who will attest?" It admits : "You may have been abetted by some ancestral spirit of revenge." Only in the restrictive *may* (*génoit' an* in the Greek) lies the implication that the doer of the deed is nonetheless responsible to himself. But precisely this is characteristic of the attitude of the chorus and of the religious background of Aeschylean tragedy : that an action done at the behest of an evil destiny (in this case the curse and spirit of revenge of the House of Atreus) is still an action even though it is predetermined by the gods. It is important for the understanding of Aeschylus that his belief in the gods, in Zeus, was not shaken even when he saw crime and evil rampant in the human world which they created and had to acknowledge that the gods themselves were responsible for this. For one basic tenet of belief in the gods was that they were just; the other was that they apportioned men's destinies, just and unjust.[2] For the profoundly religious Aeschylus the justice and the omnipotence of Zeus still coexist almost without conflict. And the chorus, helpless before the ruin of the royal house, laments over the terrible demon of the dynastic curse, while at the same time relying on Zeus :

> It is a great spirit—great—
> You tell of, harsh in anger,
> A ghastly tale, alas,
> Of unsatisfied disaster

Brought by Zeus, by Zeus,
Cause and worker of all.
For without Zeus what comes to pass among us?
Which of these things is outside Providence?[3]

Here, still within the bounds of faith—or, one might say, of theodicy—the question constantly posed by ethics is touched upon after all : are man's actions free or predetermined, that is to say, more or less unconsciously dictated by forces, laws, limitations which he as an individual does not control? Even Clytemnestra's deed, abominable and execrable in itself, may have been determined, in accordance with the will of higher powers, by a curse irrevocably pronounced by the gods, whose reasons are inscrutable to man. In Aeschylus there is still no opposition to evil fate and divine decrees; only in Euripides does this begin to make itself heard.

But if we read a question of this sort into the Aeschylean text, we must realize that this still does not establish any facts about this poet's intentions. We cannot simply say that Aeschylus wanted to present the problem of free will, of man's responsibility or non-responsibility for his actions as such. We can only draw inferences from what the text says and from what is often present but unformulated in the text. Our standpoint is the one that will so far as possible guide our comparative study : to discover what germs the Greek dramas contain for the modern interpretations of their themes. In doing this we are not modernizing the classical work itself but rather trying to uncover the archaic form of the human problems whose nature makes them perennially topical.

Freedom or predetermination of action becomes thematic for the first time in the treatment of the Orestes story. So far as Clytemnestra is concerned, the poet makes it clear enough that her reference to the dynastic curse is nothing but an excuse; she breathes a sigh of relief, so to speak, when the chorus reacts positively to it. She is the murderer of her husband; the crucial thing is her deed itself.

To make this clear, to bring it home to the audience in tangible reality, is the function of the Agamemnon play within the *Oresteia* as a whole. Once Clytemnestra had been definitively established in this form, she was incorporated into the story of Orestes and Electra in the vast majority of subsequent interpretations of the Atridae theme. This means that her deed serves merely as prehistory, existing in the memory of the active characters, including herself, and referred to by them. Hence, however strongly Clytemnestra is accentuated and motivated in the Orestes and Electra plays, our study must consider this figure, definitively created by Aeschylus, in relation to the problems of her children.

This also applies to Gerhart Hauptmann's tetralogy on the House of Atreus, even though it too includes a separate Clytemnestra play entitled *Agamemnon's Death,* for, as we shall see later, this play's whole function and significance rest on the great complex of the Iphigenia story. More or less the same thing applies to O'Neill's modernized adaptation of the Electra theme, in which Clytemnestra's relationship to Electra (or Christine Mannon's to Lavinia) received its most extreme treatment. Alfieri's *Agamemnon,* as we have said, represents a slightly different case; here Clytemnestra's passionate love for the unworthy Aegisthus is developed into a drama of mental suffering which humanizes the figure. Moreover, her relationship to her children shows a dominant trait of genuine maternal love, which is reciprocated by Electra. Yet Alfieri did not treat Clytemnestra's destiny as an isolated episode either, but followed it, in 1786, with an *Orestes.* For in this cycle of themes the murder of the husband always anticipates the matricide, and the problem of Orestes and Electra supersedes that of Clytemnestra.

We shall meet Clytemnestra again in these other contexts. Let us try now to develop the Orestes problem of the matricide as a logical outcome of Clytemnestra's murder of her husband.

2

ORESTES

The second play of Aeschylus' *Oresteia, The Libation Bearers,* admirably develops the situation of Agamemnon's children, Orestes and his sister Electra (ten years his senior), in a human and psychological rather than a strictly dramatic manner. The first important aspect of the play is that the members of this generation of the House of Atreus, Iphigenia as well as Electra and Orestes, are strikingly different from their parents and forebears. It is as though in their generation the curse upon the house had run its course. All three of them are innocent, pure, and loving. We shall see how Aeschylus prevents the still necessary deed of matricide from engendering another murder, another curse, as the earlier crimes did, and how later versions solve this problem.

Let us look at the problem of Orestes as presented in *The Libation Bearers,* the drama of the matricide. When Agamemnon went to war and Clytemnestra took Aegisthus as her lover, Orestes, still a child, was sent away to his cousin, King Strophius, to be brought up with the latter's son Pylades. And Orestes, the least involved of all the characters, is the one charged with avenging his father. For the law of the blood vengeance is valid, and the idea is still powerful that the soul of a murdered man demands revenge by his legitimate heir. As Wilamowitz-Moellendorff put it : "He is the will-less instrument of the dead man's soul. It acts through him."[1] If he fails in his terrible duty, there looms before him :

. . .the dark arrow of the dead men underground
from those within my blood who fell and turn to call
upon me; madness and empty terror in the night
on one who sees clear and whose eyes move in the dark,
must tear him loose and shake him until, with all his bulk
degraded by the bronze-loaded lash, he lose his city.[2]

This passage occurs in Orestes' speech at the beginning of *The Libation Bearers* in which he describes his desperate plight to Electra. The situation is this : Orestes has come to Argos with Pylades to exact vengeance. He first visits his father's grave to lay upon it a lock of hair, the offering to the dead. Here he meets Electra, accompanied by her maidservants, who compose the chorus. Electra has also come to make a sacrifice to the dead, at Clytemnestra's bidding—and therefore most unwillingly. In all Orestes and Electra plays, this meeting of the long separated brother and sister (which is also a recognition scene since in the intervening time Orestes has grown from a child into a man) is the point of departure for the action and the setting for the explication, presentation, and unfolding of their psychological situations, which are entirely different in the two cases.

Let us disregard Electra's situation for the moment and try to outline that of Orestes. For him the law of blood vengeance holds, but it is backed by the god, Loxias Apollo, of whom he says : " The mighty oracle of Loxias will not forsake me." Taken in its context of Orestes' passionate speech, this is an expression not of faith in the god but above all of his own bitter sense of outrage. Apollo was one of the most problematical deities in Greek mythology, the god of light and art, " the most spiritual of all the gods," the " founder of orders,"[3] but he was also the god of the Delphic oracle, which, far from being light, was often very dark indeed, intervening in men's destinies and leading them astray and into misfortune through its obscure pronouncements. A most unpredictable god, upon whom Euripides, dramatist of an age which had grown critical, was to declare war. But even in Aeschylus, in *The Eumenides,* Apollo had to yield to Athena in the end. This yielding is already linked to the problem of man's emerging awareness of himself, his free will, and his deliberate decisions.

This was the problem, and never was it revealed more starkly than in Orestes' situation. His terrible position of being forced to

kill his mother to avenge his father becomes even more precarious—
and indeed inescapable within the religion of Aeschylus—through
the fact that in addition to the unwritten law's being binding in
itself, Apollo has commanded him to execute it and sent him back
to Argos for this purpose. Neither the law nor the god's command
is eliminated by the fact that the exacting of blood vengeance
involves a crime of equal seriousness against Orestes' mother, that,
having committed matricide, he is pursued by the Furies, ostracized
by his fellow men, driven from his country, deprived of his
inheritance and his throne. This is his predicament.

We can of course interpret Apollo's command, the Furies, and
the outward tribulations which await Orestes as a still-archaic
symbolization in material terms of a conflict situation determined
by circumstances; but even so the conflict situation remains the true
thematic problem. The circumstances, the law of blood vengeance,
still form the primary determining factor, the compulsory situation,
compared to which Apollo's command is merely the executive
agency, so to speak, carrying out the law. This comes out very
clearly in Orestes' words after he has committed the deed:

> But while
> I hold some grip still on my wits, I say publicly
> to my friends: I killed my mother not without some right.
> My father's murder stained her, and the gods' disgust.
> As for the spells that charmed me to such daring, I
> give you in chief the seer of Pytho, Loxias. He
> declared I could do this and not be charged with wrong.
> Of my evasion's punishment I will not speak:
> no archery could hit such height of agony.   (p. 130)

Yet this is a giant step toward grappling with the problem of
guilt, as we can see from the conditional form in which the god's
word is rendered in the reference to his oracle: "I should not be
held guilty" (*Chrésant' emoí práxanti men taut' èktós aìtías kakés
einai*), which clearly implies a doubt regarding the truth of the
statement. Actually, mistrust of the god's promise of expiation has
already given way to the certainty that expiation, guiltlessness, does
not exist. Even before this attempt to justify himself, in a spontaneous reaction to his deed, Orestes calls to witness Agamemnon's
death robe with its faded bloodstains, and cries in anguish:

Now I can praise him, now I can stand by to mourn
and speak before this web that killed my father; yet
I grieve for the thing done, the death, and all our race.
I have won; but my victory is soiled, and has no pride.   (p. 129)

There are some famous lines of German poetry which sound
as though they might have been written to formulate in the most
concise and decisive way Orestes' situation, which is the situation
of man himself at its extreme :

Ihr führt ins Leben uns hinein,
Ihr lasst den Armen schuldig werden;
Dann überlasst ihr ihn der Pein;
Denn alle Schuld rächt sich auf Erden.

You lead us into life,
You let the poor man incur guilt.
Then you abandon him to torment,
For all guilt finds retribution on earth.

This is the second verse of the harpist's song from Goethe's *Wilhelm
Meister*. The *you* with which it begins refers to the "heavenly
powers" in the line of the preceding verse : "He knows you not, you
heavenly powers!" These lines seem to be imbued with the ancient
spirit of the *Oresteia*. But they can also be interpreted in the light
of modern existential philosophy, of Heidegger's description of
human existence, one of the fundamental elements of which is
that "being guilty is a kind of being which belongs to existence
itself."[4]

Even these few references enable us to identify one of the germs
in classical tragedy out of which the modern interpretations could
grow. But let us look more closely. Both Goethe and Heidegger use
the word *guilt*, and although in *The Libation Bearers* the law of
blood vengeance and Apollo's command, and later on the Furies
and the torment, stand before us as concretizations and materializa-
tions of the powers that create the condition in which Orestes will
find himself, there are also other texts, even here, which point away
from such archaic notions toward the condition of man as such.
It is of course the chorus that pronounces these thoughts :

There is no mortal man who shall turn
unhurt his life's course to an end not marred.
There is trouble here. There is more to come.

(Libation Bearers, p. 129)

"You let the poor man incur guilt. Then you abandon him to
torment." And when Goethe continues : "All guilt finds retribution
on earth," it is clear that the torment itself (the *mochthos* of the
Aeschylean chorus) represents the retribution for incurring guilt,
indeed for man's *having* to become guilty.

Heidegger's existential philosophy universalizes this situation
even more. It exists as such, implicit in man's situation in relation
to his fellows. For it can happen that even without infringing law
and justice man may somehow become guilty toward his fellowman,
even if only by encroaching on his existence, "by being guilty of the
other's becoming endangered in his existence, led astray, or even
ruined" *(Sein und Zeit,* p. 282). That "being guilty is a kind of
being which belongs to existence itself" is posited even more
universally, and without reference to the other, as a basic existential
situation consisting in the fact that *Dasein* (which in Heidegger
means man in his specific existential consciousness) is understood
as meaning "thrown," that is, as having "been brought into its
'there' but *not* of its own accord" (p. 284). This "thrownness" means
that one is constantly standing between the one and the other, being
forced to choose between them—a choice which does indeed
represent "freedom" but only insofar as the choice of the one
possibility implies "tolerating one's not having chosen the other
and not being able to choose it" (p. 285). Clearly, in this generality
of guilt there is no longer any question of vengeance, torment, or sin.

It was not Heidegger but Sartre, the dramatizer of existentialist ideas, who turned back to the Orestes model—in marked
opposition to Heidegger. But even Heidegger's description of the
existential guilt and choice situation, which makes no reference at
all to concrete ethical or psychological conditions, may call to mind
the Orestes of Greek antiquity. Forced to incur guilt toward his
mother in order to avoid guilt toward his father, and in either case
forced to tolerate the "not having chosen the other possibility and
the inability to choose it," Orestes is the concrete, material model
of a whole complex of existential problems which are still discernible
even in the blandest conventionality of contemporary life, but which

also reveal themselves, saturated with all the original conflicts, in cases where life is heading into extreme situations. These cases we sometimes call "tragic."

As we know, the legend does not want Orestes left in his desperate situation but insists that he be purged of sin. This means that the guilt situation, the compulsory incurring of guilt, is not to be acknowledged. The way this problem of expiation and redemption has been handled in the various interpretations and reinterpretations of the Orestes figure demonstrates more clearly than anything else the changes in intellectual climate from epoch to epoch.

Aeschylus presents his solution in the third play of the *Oresteia*, *The Eumenides*. At first this solution comes as a surprise to our conception of dramatic and human conflicts, which is why we find it somehow unsatisfactory. It becomes clear that Aeschylus was no longer concerned with the problem of Orestes himself but with a universal problem of human history : the problem of the state and of a just and moral order of society, now including man's autonomy, his freedom, and his independence of divine control. He presents this idea in a splendid argument among the gods, involving Apollo, Athena, and the Furies. The scene has shifted from the human to the divine sphere. The Furies have surrounded Orestes in Apollo's shrine at Delphi, where he has taken sanctuary, for Apollo, having charged him with the deed, is obliged to shelter him. The Furies surround him but they are asleep, snoring atrociously. Being powerless in the house of Apollo, they must leave their prey in peace. And now they are to be stripped of their power altogether. It is not enough that Apollo can—as he does—order them out of his shrine. It is characteristic of this extraordinary play that they are not driven out by a simple assertion of authority; they too must be reconciled and transformed. This means that the spirit of the times must change; an archaic barbarian age must yield to a new, more humane one. For although the Furies were deities, they were not Olympian goddesses but daughters of Night, lower, chthonian divinities of the underworld, upholders of crude, ancient justice like the law of blood vengeance which they called the law of the universe, binding in perpetuity. Yet Apollo, an Olympian, also ordered blood vengeance. What is the situation here?

The careful way Aeschylus articulates the moral conditions of human society as personified by the gods, then questions and resolves them, is beyond praise. Apollo and the Furies argue whether the murder of mother or husband is a greater crime. The Furies pursued the matricide but not the husband-killer, whereas Apollo for his part ordered the killing of the mother. What is behind this? Why do the Furies appear as spirits avenging the mother but not the husband? On the other hand, why does Apollo avenge the husband? Chthonian concepts are involved. The chthonian is that which is earthly, rooted in flesh and blood, which has not yet been purified by the higher forces of the spirit, of reason, but opposes them. The mother principle is the blood principle—only matricide, say the Furies, is murder of blood kindred. On the other hand, Apollo, who punishes the murder of the husband but protects the murderer of the mother, although he must necessarily be the one to carry out the punishment, points to higher human bonds than those of mere blood kinship—bonds which man assumes through his own free will and desire. He speaks of marriage and of Hera, the goddess of marriage, who represents this higher moral community of man and woman :

> You have made into a thing of no account, no place,
> The sworn faith of Zeus and of Hera, lady
> of consummations, and Cypris by such argument
> is thrown away, outlawed, and yet the sweetest things
> in man's life come from her, for married love between
> man and woman is bigger than oaths, guarded by right
> of nature.[5]

But even this defense of marriage is not enough. Apollo, although an Olympian, is still not a completely purified god here, since he ordered blood vengeance for the husband-killing. As lord of the Delphic oracle he represents another element—and a determining one—in man's non-freedom. He has to yield to Athena, who, endowed with greater insight and resolution than any of the other divinities, initiates the new, humane age. The action moves from Delphi to her city of Athens, where the legal dispute about Orestes is to be settled. And now comes the important point. Athena does not pronounce the verdict herself; human society constitutes itself a state governed by law and exercises jurisdiction, independently of the verdict of the gods, over what happens within its precincts. Athena appoints a council of citizen judges whose authority is to be valid for all time. Even the gods are to be subject to this tribunal; in the vote which follows they too cast their pebbles into the urn. Since the number of votes for and against Orestes is equal, he is pronounced free of guilt. As to the Erinyes, Athena convinces them of the blessing of such a system of justice and in this way the goddesses of vengeance become the Eumenides, benevolent deities.

This solution must be accepted in the spirit in which it was conceived by Aeschylus, the first tragedian, the glorifier of Athens, whose concern was to bring about a political and human order increasingly free of archaic belief. But so far as the Orestes problem is concerned, this solution is unsatisfactory, for the problem is left unresolved. The vote may have exonerated Orestes, but this is what Kant would call a legal but not a moral decision. Orestes did not decide for himself whether his deed had to be committed or not. He was not able to act as a free man making up his own mind; neither did he as a free man freely atone for his guilt. He is acquitted over his own head, not on grounds which he himself gives but in accordance with impersonal laws to which he contributes nothing. In other words, Orestes still remains a problem, a model of man non-free in the true sense, predestined in his actions—until Sartre tackles the problem afresh and brings it to a solution, the germ of which, however, is already present in Aeschylus and even more strongly in Euripides.

Euripides treated the Orestes problem in a most remarkable way, particularly from the modern point of view. His *Electra,* written in 413 B.C., and his *Orestes,* written in 408, survive. Comparing them, especially comparing the ending of the *Electra* with the later *Orestes,* we cannot dismiss the idea that Euripides himself may not have been satisfied with the solution in the earlier play, and even with his treatment of the Orestes figure, and therefore tackled the problem again. At the end of the *Electra,* after the matricide, the inner impossibility of the deed is presented more outspokenly than in Aeschylus and much more so than in Sophocles' *Electra.* In *The Libation Bearers* the chief factor in Orestes' despair is the misery in store for him. Euripides' Orestes is overcome with horror at the deed itself; now for the first time he becomes terribly aware that it is his mother he has killed. The chorus cries :

> Weep for destiny; destiny yours
> to mother unforgettable wrath,
> to suffer unforgettable pain
> beyond pain at your children's hands.
> You paid for their father's death as the law asks.[6]

But this attempt to explain and excuse is weak and leads at once into Orestes' accusation of Apollo :

> Phoebus, you hymned the law in black
> melody, but the deed has shone
> white as a scar.   (p. 59)

Orestes' self-accusation and his burden of guilt are emphasized for the audience and made real as a state of heartfelt anguish when he goes over the ghastly scene again for himself and Electra : how his mother uncovered her breast, laid her hand on his chin—the traditional gesture of imploring mercy—and clung to his neck, how the blade fell from his hands and he dissolved in grief. Now, however, this psychological situation is cut short and the guilt problem settled much as Aeschylus settled it, and of course following his model. Hovering over the palace roof appear the brother demigods Castor and Pollux. They send Orestes to Athens to be freed of his guilt by the tribunal, which is to acquit him of the murder because Apollo, having ordered it, assumes the blame. (He did not act justly, say the Dioscuri, but Apollo is their lord and they keep silent. We may realize, not without amusement, that human situations, even among gods and demigods, tend to be much the same.)

Yet it looks as though this quick happy ending to the Orestes problem did not satisfy Euripides, and this is borne out by the *Orestes* he wrote five years later. Evidently what interested him was not the solution but the aftereffects of such a deed on a human mind. Euripides' *Orestes* is not considered one of his masterpieces, and it is not often cited among the *Oresteia* plays. Unquestionably it betrays a certain coarsening, not to say a brutality, which has been taken for a decline in the art of the drama. Nevertheless, this tragedy, one of the last Euripides wrote, is of great interest. It penetrates more intensely than any other treatment of the story into the desperate psychological situation of the matricide, shrinking from nothing, not even from brutality, in displaying it. For this, as a closer look proves, is the face of reality.

Euripides places Orestes after the murder squarely within his own reality, and he does this in a twofold way. He leaves him alone with his own anguished mind, deprived of the help of the gods. We find him, not in the sheltering sanctuary of Apollo, as in Aeschylus, but—and this is entirely realistically seen—in his own environment, within his family in his own city of Argos, of which he is now the ruler. In this way Euripides creates a situation of both internal and external duress, a situation which can deprive a man of his reason and drive him to actions which show that he is no longer in control of himself.

The persecution by the Furies, treated more realistically than ever before, is completely internalized and shown as psychological in origin and pathological in appearance. Although they are still called goddesses of vengeance, the Furies actually are symbols and names for the pangs of conscience, rather than existing beings :

> Goddesses of terror,
> runners on the wind,
> revelers of sorrow
> whose rites are tears!
> Women of darkness
> Eumenides whose wings
> shiver the taut air,
> demanding blood,
> avengers of murder,
> we implore you—
> release this boy,
> Agamemnon's son,
> from madness of murder,
> the blood that whirls him on![7]

Orestes is shown not fleeing from men, as the traditional legend had it, but in his ancestral palace at Argos, where the family has assembled, as it naturally would after such events. Not only Electra is present, but Helen too and her daughter Hermione. Menelaus arrives, and Helen's grandfather, Tyndareus. The people of Argos are there too, playing an important part. This creates a convincing picture of Orestes' situation, of outer and inner threats converging upon him. Man is shown not merely alone with himself or with the gods, but in the position of a citizen, a man among his fellow-men, a *zoon politikon*, and that means in this case that the deed has external as well as internal consequences. A poor, terrified Orestes, tearing his own flesh in remorse, clings to Electra and to Menelaus. Euripides excels at stark portrayals of human anguish. Orestes raves wildly, accusing himself, Electra, and the god :

> I know, you consented to the murder too,
> But I killed, not you.
> > No—
> I accuse Apollo.   (p. 129)

One understands this effort, useless as always, to seek the causes of one's own deed elsewhere, in circumstances, in other people; and beneath the layer of mythological impersonations Euripides makes it transparent, after all, that the skein of life, the relationships which every man has, can become so tangled that guilt and innocence, too, can no longer be clearly separated. One might say that for Euripides this is the sorrow of life.

A realism of a more nihilistic tinge now begins to pervade this play. Orestes and Electra find themselves threatened from outside as well as inwardly. A faction of Argives, in rebellion against them and refusing to recognize the matricide as king, has set up a tribunal which is supposed to condemn them both to death. An undeniable weakness of the play is that Orestes at once thinks of nothing but saving himself, and in doing so he continues on the path of crime (or more properly, he now really enters upon it). His despairing conscience and his instinct of self-preservation do not seem to fuse into a unified personality; that is to say, the poet seems to have failed to create a consistent character. This has to be admitted, but the very admission says something about the tragedy as a whole, which in this respect differs essentially from that of Sophocles. Unlike Sophocles, Euripides is not concerned with moral decisions or with the upholding of human dignity in the inimical contingencies and constellations of life or with portraying human greatness. His major concern is an unprejudiced, not to say pitiless, exposure of human life, of the human condition, the soul and the instincts, man's weakness rather than his strength. Unquestionably Orestes is presented in this play as a weak man in conflict with himself, and in this way Euripides brought out the essence of the Orestes figure in a more consistent, realistic way than previous versions had done. This seems to be the central motive of this undeniably distasteful Orestes play.

The events which Euripides sets forth with this motive in mind (or which must at least be interpreted in its light) are as follows. Orestes seeks help against the citizens of Argos from his uncle Menelaus, believing him to be under a greater obligation than anybody else to provide it since it was for the sake of his shameless wife that the whole cycle of misfortune and crime began. We cannot say for sure whether Orestes' almost cynically calculating attitude, his striving to save his own life, is an intentional trait, whether Euripides intended to make him a weak personality, yielding to every influence, which is how he impresses us in this play and how legendary tradition has implicitly shown him. Be that as it may, it is clear that for Euripides the strength of the life instinct in Orestes, despite his deed, which has made his life not worth living, has become a model of man's difficult and rationally incomprehensible nature and situation.[8] Not accidentally did Euripides create a Medea who kills her children, nor is it by accident that in his last, almost monstrous work, *The Bacchae*, written immediately after the *Orestes* and first performed after his death, he took as his theme the terrible power of Dionysus, the bacchantic frenzy of an old woman, Queen Agave, the mother who tears her own son to pieces.

Orestes becomes more and more lost, pulled this way and that. The role of Pylades was introduced for this express purpose. He instigates a devilish plan. After it becomes clear that the citizens of Argos intend to make good their threats, and Orestes' life is seen to be forfeit, they can at least destroy another life. By killing Helen they will take revenge upon Menelaus, the legendary weakling and cuckold, who has faintheartedly retreated. If he exacts vengeance, it will then be Hermione's turn to be the victim. These wild schemes may be seen as last resorts, counsels of desperation, in which every decision as to right and wrong fails. The action now shows their execution, insofar as it is in the power of Orestes, Electra, and Pylades. For they fail right at the outset, with Helen, who can never be killed because her myth of divine-mortal birth as daughter of Zeus and Leda precludes it. At the moment of greatest danger she is therefore saved by Apollo, freed for ever from her earthly ties, and set beside her brothers, Castor and Pollux, in the heavens as a guiding star, the tutelary goddess of sailors.

And now Apollo intervenes, as he did in Euripides' *Electra*, in the hopeless chaos which he has helped to create. But Euripides makes a far weaker attempt than Aeschylus to provide a solution from within. Apollo puts only the external circumstances in order. As in the *Electra*, Aeschylus' solution is adopted, inasmuch as Orestes is sent to Athens to be exonerated. But even this ending is not happy enough. Orestes receives Hermione in marriage and lives happily ever after as King of Argos; Electra gets Pylades, as she does in the earlier play, and only Menelaus is left out in the cold.

It is almost impossible to say to what extent this superficial solution should be regarded as a deliberate conceptual element of the play. The *deus* or *dea ex machina* is certainly characteristic of Euripides' drama. He nearly always unties the knot, resolves the confused situation, through the intervention of a deity just at the point where it has to take a turn for the better—for example, if the legend requires it. At a deeper level, though, this reliance on the gods to put everything right at the eleventh hour is an antique mode of expression for Euripides' very realism, rather than an expression of religious faith in divine benevolence (like the Christian faith, for example). This is borne out by the whole character of Euripides' work, which is critical of the gods. That the gods act so arbitrarily, involving man in involuntary sin but then again expiating him and allowing him to live, may be taken as a skeptical insight into the arbitrariness of life, in which man's own power is very limited, very relative. In *Iphigenia in Tauris,* Orestes puts it in these words :

> Even the Gods, with all Their name for wisdom,
> Have only dreams and lies and lose Their course,
> Blinded, confused, and ignorant as we.[9]

Confusion reigns—confusion over man's difficult position in the world; the Orestes of Euripides is almost an exemplary model of Heidegger's "being thrown" into the world.

It is not surprising that the Orestes theme should have challenged very modern writers, that the constellation of personages, types, and characters in the story should over and over again have inspired such a diversity of dramatic works based on this pattern. So far as Orestes is concerned, we have thus far considered only those classical plays in which his problem is the central one, however closely it may be linked with Electra's problem by the nature of the plot. But the character of Orestes established by Aeschylus and particularly by Euripides certainly has something to do with the fact that in the later literary history of the Oresteia he is no longer the central figure but appears as a comparison figure flanked by his sisters Electra and Iphigenia, though he remains of course indispensable to action and conflict. He is always the matricide, driven by guilt, not freely taking action but having to take it on account of his crime, one who is driven, defined, made to suffer by it—and thus in need of salvation. The most extreme portrayal in world literature of the suffering man in need of redemption and redeemed may well be the Orestes of Goethe's *Iphigenie,* the completely passive man seeking refuge in madness, redeemed, calmed, and restored from his pathological state by his sister's "pure humanity."

Not until Sartre's *Les Mouches (The Flies)* will the character of Orestes as delineated in Greek antiquity be radically transformed. Indeed, here it is turned into its opposite. Sartre's play is in deliberate opposition to the traditional view of the Orestes problem; hence the revolutionary changes in the theme and the plot. We may add that the form of Sartre's play also represents a radical reshaping not of the classical Greek tragedies alone but of all plays on Greek themes that had so far appeared in literature. Yet we must not go too far in linking the formal change to the transformation of the theme. One might well put it the other way around and say that the classical story has been given the prose form of the modern French theatre, which is its general form for all themes, classical or not. Thus Sartre's *The Flies* is formally no different from the Greek plays of Giraudoux and Anouilh. The elimination of the form and style of high tragedy characterizes all of them. Prose, common speech in fact, the dropping of archaisms, the use—not just uninhibited but quite deliberate—of modern vocabulary and stage settings while retaining the ancient plot, time, and place— this is what makes the action and meaning of these plays flash back and forth between antiquity and modern times in a way that holds distinct potentialities for parody of the kind Giraudoux used so effectively in his *Electra.*

Sartre, however, is no parodist. He is a rigorous ethicist. Not by chance did he choose the Oresteia as a theme. *The Flies* appeared in 1943, the same year as his major philosophical work *L'Etre et le*

Néant (*Being and Nothingness*); it presents an exemplary documentation of a crux of his philosophy : the theory of freedom. Orestes' situation in the Greek tragedies suggests that a philosophy of freedom might find his story a most rewarding subject for poetic and dramatic treatment. Sartre answered the agonizing question of man's freedom or lack of freedom, of his predestined situation, by cutting the Gordian knot of this situation—the "you let the poor man incur guilt," the "being guilty as a kind of being which belongs to existence itself,"—with the sword of his philosophy of freedom.

Without beating about the bush, he goes straight to the point at which the traditional Orestes problem had remained unresolved. He takes up the problem of the gods—or what amounts to the same thing, the problem of God—and confronts man with it. Let us look back to Euripides, where the germ of Sartre's formulation of the problem is most clearly visible. His Orestes does indeed revolt against Apollo for plunging man into guilt, but—and this is the decisive point—without ever losing faith in the gods. Faith falters and skepticism rears its head when the gods appear hostile or lacking in understanding, but it is immediately restored when they are helpful and deliver man from guilt and suffering. How does Euripides' Orestes phrase it at the end, when Apollo has straightened everything out?

> Hail, Apollo,
> for your prophetic oracles! True prophet,
> not false!
> And yet, when I heard you speak,
> I thought I heard the whispers of some fiend
> speaking through your mouth.
> But all is well,
> and I obey.[10]

This shows that for all the guilt and suffering inherent in existence, man, as the tragedians and even the skeptical Euripides depict him, still does not feel himself alone, abandoned by the gods, thrown back upon himself. So long as "heavenly powers" can be invoked and held responsible man is still sheltered within the security of faith and transcendence. Faith may be lost, but it is lost only to be found again. Even for Goethe, the only meaning of human history lay in the struggle between belief and disbelief. Man is alone and unsheltered only when faith no longer exists, when God is dead, to use Nietzsche's words. Instead of the knowledge and feeling of sheltering security, anxiety becomes "the basic character of existence," as Heidegger saw and formulated it, anxiety, which fears "the inner-worldly nothing and nowhere" (*Sein und Zeit,* p. 186). This is the state of insecurity pure and simple. Heidegger uses the term *unheimlich,* uncanny, referring back to its original German sense of "not at home" or "not having a home" (p. 188).

What does Sartre make of all this? We shall see that for him these existential concepts of anxiety, being guilty, and insecurity are purged of their negative, threatening, sinister, uncanny character and turned into something positive. Sartre's existentialism might in fact be said to turn in unspoken opposition against Heidegger's since it harbors and nurtures the germ of an idealistic ethic. So far as Orestes is concerned, one might suppose that Sartre takes up where Euripides left off. Sartre's Orestes too holds the gods responsible for allowing man to become guilty. But Sartre goes much farther, not only farther than Euripides but beyond any previous interpretation of this attitude toward life, farther even than the atheists themselves. In Sartre the gods are unmasked, accused of keeping man's feeling of guilt and anxiety alive for the sake of their own power and sovereignty. For only the man who is tormented by guilt and anxiety needs the gods—needs God. The god who appears in Sartre is not Apollo but, characteristically, a Zeus, a Jupiter, father of the gods, who stands transparently, as the other Olympians never could, for the one god, the Judeo-Christian God, and ultimately for the idea of God itself.

The Jupiter of *The Flies* is by no means in the dark about the exclusively human—all too human—basis on which his power rests. He is well satisfied with the murder of Agamemnon committed long ago, "What a profit I made on it! For one dead man, twenty thousand others overcome with repentance—that's the balance sheet. It wasn't a bad bargain."[11] But Jupiter says this to Aegisthus, the murderer, who is nonetheless now king of Argos. And this is the whole point. For Aegisthus too knows what is what; he is plainly in league with Jupiter. He too must vigilantly maintain his power. At the same time he is an extremely guilty man, living in fear that retribution will overtake him some day. In tacit connivance with Jupiter, in fact prompted by him, he has therefore devised a very subtle scheme for keeping constantly alive the guilt feeling of the citizens of Argos, who here symbolize mankind. Everyone has incurred guilt sometime, somewhere. As the chorus says in Aeschylus : " No man's life can run its course unsullied." But this is now turned into the existentialist principle that what matters is not concrete, compact guilt, not the fact of having committed a wrong, but feeling guilty as such, as a mode of existence.

Every year Aegisthus and Clytemnestra—as well they might— organize a festival of the dead at which the poor people of Argos are told that their dead relatives will appear to charge them with the injustice which they in some way did to them long ago. A guilt and anxiety psychosis grips the city, and the flies, that is, the degraded Furies, feast like vultures on a battlefield. "I stink! I stink!" cry the people. "I am a revolting piece of carrion. Look, the flies are thick on me as crows. Sting, gouge, bore, you avenging flies. Worm your way through my flesh right to my filthy heart. I have sinned. I have sinned a hundred thousand times. I am a sewer, a cesspool" (p. 50). Aegisthus and Clytemnestra revel in this sight, for this is their way of making their own great concrete guilt disappear in the mass psychosis and at the same time keeping the people in subjection. Those who are not free inwardly will not set themselves free outwardly either, and so far as Jupiter and his business are concerned, his interests are identical with those of the ruling couple : those twenty thousand guilt- and remorse-ridden men are the profit he reaps from the ancient deed of Aegisthus and Clytemnestra. This is indeed a clever invention, both for the meaning of the play and for the development of its more than obvious symbolism and metaphorical sense. The festival of the dead is, or stands for, the demonstration of man's non-freedom, of his existential situation itself.

Orestes now appears in this afflicted city—an Orestes who, in radical contrast to the traditional Orestes, is a free man, free, that is, from any tie to the gods, a free man who sees through the gods and whom Jupiter must fear. It is very characteristic indeed that this Orestes has not come to Argos in response to law or divine decree but as a stranger who does not hear about the murder until he is at the very spot where it took place. But the news is far from inspiring thoughts of blood vengeance. The blood vengeance motif does not appear any more, and this removes the factor which formerly determined the situation. All action is man's free choice and decision. Certainly Orestes will kill Clytemnestra and Aegisthus, not to comply with the law of blood vengeance but to deliver from its tormentors this afflicted city, whose people, dressed in their shabby, dreary mourning clothes, are preparing for the terrible festival of the dead. Even before he meets Electra, before the recognition scene, he has his argument with Jupiter, in which the decisive ideas propounded by this play of ideas are stated. It is a typical Sartre invention to present this god, already half stripped of his godhead, as a most skeptical god, who is all too aware of the shaky basis of his power and who therefore does not think particularly highly of human beings or, for that matter, of himself. When, disguised in human shape, he tells Orestes of Agamemnon's murder, he seems to dismiss with a shrug these people of Argos for whom a crime of this sort is just a break in the tedium of existence, who even take a voluptuous pleasure in it. This god knows that he lives not by the faith of higher human minds but by their baseness and corruption, by their need for him as a last refuge in their despair, anxiety, and guilt.

This Jupiter is a nihilistic despiser of men. He assumes features which in Christian symbolism belong to the devil. In fact, Sartre's atheism reaches its peak in the play to which he gave the title *Le Diable et le Bon Dieu* (*The Devil and the Good Lord*), whose hero, Götz von Berlichingen, personifies evil, the devil, in the first part and good, God, in the second. But the evil man is not God's adversary and absolute opposite, as the title might suggest; God too appears as a power whose works look little different from those of the devil to suffering humanity. What do these atheistic symbols mean? They mean opposition—opposition to the positing of any extra-human authorities of any kind. For Sartre such authorities are nothing but expressions of man's non-freedom and hence his lack of human dignity.

We have now reached the point where we can recognize the radical turn Sartre has imposed upon the Orestes problem. Given that belief in the gods signifies sheltered security and that man is alone, exposed, and insecure only when he loses this faith, Sartre now transforms the insecurity of aloneness, the negation of transcendence, into something positive, into the strength and the power which men acquire from this very insecurity, that is to say, into a freedom to which Sartre, for this very reason, could consider man condemned. "Man is free. Man is freedom," he says in *L'existentialisme est un humanisme* (*Existentialism and Humanism*), which was written about the same time as *The Flies* and is its theoretical counterpart. "We have nothing behind us, nothing ahead of us in the bright realm of values, of justifications or excuses. We are alone, without excuses. This I express in the words : Man is condemned to freedom. Once thrown into the world, he is answerable for everything he does."[12] This sentence expresses the dialectical relationship in the structure of freedom which, being fundamentally existential, for that very reason takes an idealistic turn : existential insofar as it derives from being "thrown into the world," idealistic insofar as self-responsibility is implicit in this "thrownness." Orestes can tell Jupiter that he may be the king of the gods, the rocks, and the stars, but he is not the king of men. The dialectical problem of man as a created being, even if he must regard himself as created by God, narrows down to this : he is a creature created as a free being. When Jupiter demands in anger : "So I am not your king, you impudent worm? Who, then, created you?" Orestes can reply : "You." But he adds : "But you should not have made me free" (p. 111). And mankind is, so to speak, wholly divorced from the godhead when Orestes, with irrefutable logic, points out to Jupiter that the moment he created him a free being he no longer created him as his own creature. "I *am* my freedom. No sooner did you create men than I ceased to belong to you" (p. 111). Now man's freedom consists in his capacity and opportunity to choose his actions and, having made his choice, to be answerable for them.

We recognize the turn Sartre is giving to the traditional Orestes theme and we see how productive this element is going to prove in demonstrating and illustrating his activist philosophy of freedom. Sartre changes the Orestes of antiquity, who is forced to become guilty, into one who wills to become guilty. He freely chooses his deed of matricide. He chooses it to make the idea of freedom as such triumphant. For he does not kill Clytemnestra and Aegisthus because he is bound to exact blood vengeance or to fulfil a law or a decree of the gods; he kills them because they have both committed a sin against freedom by fostering among their subjects anxiety and guilt, the very things that make men non-free.

This, however, is not the end of the Orestes problem for Sartre.

Responsibility for the choice is an inseparable adjunct of freedom of choice. Even freely chosen guilt remains guilt, producing torment and anguish in the soul. "The groans of my mother, do you think my ears will ever cease to hear them? And her tremendous eyes— two displaced oceans—in her chalky face, do you think my eyes will ever cease to see them? And the anguish that consumes you [Electra], do you think it will ever cease to gnaw at me?" (p. 103).

The flies swarm upon Orestes, never to leave him alone again. For it lies in the nature of this existentialist Oresteia that it cannot end in the traditional way. Orestes is never redeemed. For Sartre, redemption and expiation would be indications of man's non-freedom, of his dependency, since they refer him to other authorities than those he finds within himself. "But what does it matter?" Orestes continues. " I am free. Beyond anguish and memories. Free. And at one with myself" (p. 103). Even the entirely humanistic exoneration based entirely on human morality which is granted to Goethe's Orestes through the moral purity and strength of his sister —"all human shortcomings toned for by pure humanity"—would still be for Sartre a limitation of man's freedom, which resides precisely in the fact that man cannot be exonerated (that is, relieved of his burden of guilt by somebody else) but must take upon himself the guilt, and with it the curse, of his existence. This, however, eliminates every deterministic factor that might still be left in the Heideggerian conception of existential culpability. As we have said, Sartre changes the existentialist interpretation of the human condition back into an idealistic one—a reversal rooted in the very idea of freedom.

As the exposition proceeds, the application of Sartre's activistic philosophy of freedom and the continuing reversal of the tradition sharpen the Orestes problem more and more, but they also make it increasingly dubious; somehow it becomes less credible. In the end Orestes, now king of Argos, is elevated to a savior figure on the model of Jesus. He redeems the Argives, who symbolize mankind, from their anxiety and guilt. Not only does he liberate them from their tormentors who organize the festival of the dead; he adds to this concrete act one which is abstract and symbolic : he takes their guilt upon himself. "Your guilt and your remorse, your terrors in the night, the crime of Aegisthus—all these are mine. I take them upon myself. Fear your dead no longer. They are *my* dead. See :

your faithful flies have left you to come to me" (p. 120). He renounces his kingdom and goes forth from his people into the wilder-
ness. The Furies hurl themselves upon him, shrieking.

The deliverance of the people of Argos seems to contradict the
thesis of the play, which specifically rules out deliverance and
exoneration. If, as Orestes demonstrates, man is free only when he
freely takes his guilt upon himself, then the Argives, inasmuch as
they are human beings, should not be delivered but,—since they are
condemned to freedom by being men—should free themselves. To
be sure, the play demonstrates man's existential problem through
the example of Orestes and Electra, not that of the people of Argos.
The savior idea is related only to Orestes; the object of salvation is
immaterial. This idea of the savior, however, in its turn symbolizes
another element in Sartre's theory of freedom, which even goes
beyond man's responsibility for his actions and his choice : the
theory that man, in making his own choice, should choose simultaneously on behalf of all mankind. "When we say that man chooses
himself, we understand that each of us chooses himself; but we also
mean that in choosing himself he chooses all men."[13] In choosing
his own deed and his own sin, Orestes is also choosing those of all
men, represented collectively by the people of Argos. Obviously
such an abstract ethical notion, which is realizable only in the idea,
not as a concrete action, must be given at least some approximate
concrete form, some symbolic act, to give it body in the play. This
is done by turning the choice on behalf of all men, the choice of
guilt, into the act of redemption from guilt, the act of suffering for
the sake of others. But this symbol is tangible because it is given in
the religious tradition of Christianity. Orestes calls himself King of
the Argives in the sense in which Jesus is called King of the Jews.

If we look more closely, however, the Christian idea of redemption also proves to be an activistic transformation, even a reversal, of
the problem of redemption as posed by the Greek Orestes. From the
outset the idea of redemption complements the idea of sin. But
Sartre transforms the passive Orestes of antiquity, who is redeemed,
into the active redeemer. Now when a savior figure points to the
Christian savior figure, when indeed it can only be understood in
this way, then the specifically Christian savior concept is eliminated,
having been completely transformed into a humanistic conception,
as is inevitable within the framework of Sartre's philosophy. The

act of redemption is identical with the choice of assuming responsibility, the authentic "act" upon which rests man's dignity, that which makes him human. Oskar Seidlin has said that to make the matricide the savior represents "the most scandalous dehumanization and brutalization of the myth."[14] His objection is an occasion for emphasizing once more that Sartre's Oresteia must not be mistaken for a psychological play on a given traditional theme. The traditional characters and plot elements, like the ones that are his own invention, merely serve abstractly to demonstrate Sartre's philosophy of freedom. The essential thing is not the human, psychological circumstances of the matricide but Orestes' situation as a striking instance of the whole problem of freedom.

T. S. Eliot's *The Family Reunion*,[15] which should be discussed in this context, appeared four years before *The Flies*. This is a play of the same type as O'Neill's *Mourning Becomes Electra*, in which the classical model stands forth behind the contemporary characters and setting. Here again the model is the story of the Atridae, the Orestes motif, and Eliot too links it with the savior concept (although there is no reason to suppose that Sartre was influenced by Eliot). To be sure, the Orestes model emerges in a much more indirect, remote, and more alienated way than the House of Atreus motif in O'Neill's play. In fact there is at first only one factor to startle the reader or the audience and divert its train of thought from the company assembled at the Dowager Lady Monchensey's family estate toward the *Oresteia* of Greek antiquity. Twice the Furies appear in the window embrasure, visible only to the man they are pursuing, Lady Monchensey's son Harry. Why are they pursuing him? Has he come to kill his mother and avenge his father? Not at all. After eight years of obviously unhappy drifting, Lord Monchensey has come back to his ancestral home on his mother's birthday in search of peace and quiet. His mother has been eagerly awaiting his coming home to assume his position as head of the family. His aunts, his mother's sisters, his uncle, his father's brother, and the old family doctor are all assembled, waiting for Harry to arrive before they go in to dinner.

Practically nothing happens. And yet shadows of the past sometimes seem to be moving behind the scenes of the present, shadows of guilt, shadows of murders—whether actually committed or merely willed is never explicitly stated. Perhaps Harry really did push his young wife overboard during a sea voyage; perhaps she committed suicide. The shadows which darken his life lie further back : in his parents' unhappy marriage and separation, the details of which he now learns from his Aunt Agatha, a sort of Cassandra figure. He learns that his mother drove his father to his death, that his father and Agatha, with whom he was in love, had planned to kill his mother.

Although neither the plot nor the characters of the *Oresteia* are discernible as models, the text can say at one point : "Whether in Argos or in England, there are certain inflexible and unalterable laws." Eliot, with his religious bent, gives us a shadowy glimpse, behind his own play, of the web of murder and guilt in which the House of Atreus is entangled. He does this for one purpose only : to make visible the possibility of redemption, the redemption of all mankind by one man who takes upon himself the sins of all. Harry Monchensey renounces his inheritance and leaves his family—on his way to salvation. As Agatha says, he has crossed the frontier, the frontier of despair, beyond which safety and danger no longer mean what they mean to other people, the ones on this side. All this vaguely shades off into the realm of the transcendental, the religious order of the world.

The significant point is that it should be possible at all for a Christian savior concept to take the classical *Oresteia* and the figure of Orestes as its point of departure : in Sartre reshaped into an activistic idea of freedom, hence a humanistic idea; in Eliot still retaining its religious cast but so tenuously that even the germ of the redemption concept present in the *Oresteia* is no longer recognizable and only the occasional Orestes motifs, or allusions to them, remind us of Harry's connection with the antique figure. But for this very reason Eliot's play proves how seminal the Orestes problem was as it was stated in Greek tragedy and how many interpretations it will bear, all of them effective, from the most direct imitations to the most indirect of echoes.

~𝒮 3 ℰ~
ELECTRA

Sartre's *The Flies* undoubtedly represents the most striking treatment of the Orestes problem in world drama, amounting to a radical reversal of the theme of the Greek Orestes, whose actions are determined. It is therefore not surprising that the Electra figure should also be affected by this shift. She too is sharply scrutinized in the light of Sartre's idea of freedom, and in the process this astute philosopher comes up against a crux of the Electra problem which he is the first to expose, although it is inherent in this figure and in her role. For this reason it is profitable to examine the Electra problem, which has challenged so many dramatists, in the light of *The Flies*.

First, however, let us go back to the Electra figure as it was established in Greek antiquity and look at her from the point of view of freedom of action and will. We find that she is much freer than Orestes. Neither accepted custom nor, consequently, divine decree requires that Electra execute the blood vengeance, the matricide. Nobody is demanding anything of her and she could perfectly well go on living in King Aegisthus' house. The contrast she offers to Orestes from the very beginning lies in the fact that everything she does and feels has its roots in her own idiosyncratic personality. As the human personality became interesting in itself, the attention of tragedians dealing with the Oresteia theme was attracted to Electra and focused increasingly upon her.

What is her situation? Her traditional role is to encourage

Orestes to matricide, to make this irresolute man, who does not act on his own initiative or in response to his own feelings, psychologically ready to commit the unnatural act. This is also significant for the deeper motivation of Orestes' action, which becomes convincing as a truly critical conflict situation only if Orestes is not forced into it by external pressure alone. He must at least have been able to think of his mother's deed as something committed long ago of which he has no first-hand knowledge, and it must now be brought home to him in distressing, explicit immediacy. Seen in this light, Electra's role is already a master stroke of dramatic technique. She was present; she remembers; she cannot forget. Her hatred grows stronger and stronger. This element in the characterization is concretely accentuated by making her a maid in Aegisthus' house. Aeschylus first did this, and it persists in variations of all kinds down to Sartre. Euripides' variation (used again by Giraudoux) was to marry Electra to a farmer. She is always degraded in some way by those who fear her knowledge of their secrets and her hatred.

In the earliest version of the Electra figure in Aeschylus' *Libation Bearers,* her personality is not yet so explicitly profiled as in the later Greek plays on this theme. After the recognition she does indeed incite Orestes to murder, supported by the chorus of maidservants, but it is characteristic that her grieving for her father and her wish to avenge him are not unmixed with thought for her own life—not merely its present shame and degradation but its future happiness. To our way of thinking, a passage like the following one seems odd. Kneeling at the grave, the brother and sister pray to their dead father for the success of their deed and for happiness in their future life. Orestes asks his father to let him become lord of the House of Atreus. Electra joins in, asking him to grant her a house and husband when Aegisthus has been killed, and beseeching Agamemnon's compassion for son and daughter alike.* This indicates that Electra is not yet clearly defined as a character, a person, an individual. She is not yet the frenzied Electra later to be created by Sophocles, the one who has survived in literature. That Electra, the psychological profile of the Electra figure up to

*Translator's note. This interpretation of Electra's prayer diverges slightly from the text, which, as given in the Loeb translation, says: "I . . . of the fulness of my inheritance will from my father's house at my bridal offer libations unto thee" (*Libation Bearers,* lines 486-488).

and including Freud's Electra complex, we shall discuss in its proper context from Sophocles to O'Neill. Let us now skip directly to Sartre. For there exists between the still incompletely defined Electra of Aeschylus and the Electra of Sartre a connection so natural that Sartre can take something which in Aeschylus, for example, is naively expressed, recognizable, if at all, only germinally, and sharpen it into a thematic problem and documentation of human behavior.

Sartre turns the brother and sister, accomplices in this one deed, into antithetical positive and negative embodiments of his philosophy of freedom. Orestes is the free man—and we have shown how his traditional problematic situation was changed and reversed to make him so. By contrast, Electra, who is free born, so to speak, and who loves, hates, and acts purely according to her own impulses, becomes in Sartre signally non-free in her actions and therefore morally contemptible. As Sartre sees the figure and the role, Electra wants the deed done, and wants it more passionately and for more personal reasons and emotions than Orestes, but instead of performing it herself she lets somebody else do it. For this reason she becomes, as it were, suspect to Sartre.

It is interesting to note how this aspect, which has always been inherent in the Electra figure, was ignored in characterizing her before Sartre. Nevertheless a germ of it is to be found in Sophocles' Electra. Once she is convinced that Orestes is dead (for throughout the classical tradition Orestes, when he arrives at Mycenae, for tactical reasons keeps up the belief that he is dead, or allows his companion, Pylades or the tutor, to do so), she announces her resolution to kill at least Aegisthus herself:

> The deed must then be done by my own hand
> alone. For I will not leave it unfulfilled.[1]

But if we look at this passage from Sartre's viewpoint, its insertion just at this point takes on an almost symptomatic significance. Electra pronounces this decision after she has tried without success to secure the help and complicity of her sister Chrysothemis (whose function in the Electra problem will be discussed later); she is saved from having to perform the deed herself by Orestes' arrival just at that moment. Both these factors detract from or diminish Electra's readiness to commit the deed unaided.

Hofmannsthal's treatment of this factor in his *Elektra*, a free adaptation of the Sophoclean tragedy, written in 1903, shows this up even more plainly. With passionate, frantic insistence his Electra tries to persuade her sister to kill not only Aegisthus but Clytemnestra too, tries to give Chrysothemis a transfusion of her own will so to speak :

> I'll twine myself around you, sink my roots
> in you, inject my will into your blood.[2]

This drives her own part in the projected deed into the back of her mind, so that even this element of initiative which Sophocles and Hofmannsthal give her does not ultimately change the traditional Electra figure. She is still what she was in the legend : one who merely incites to murder and gets somebody else to do what she wants done. "Your task awaits you. You have drawn first chance at spilling blood," she says unequivocally in Euripides.

Sartre takes this as his starting point. His Electra exemplifies humanly weak, base, that is to say, non-free behavior as plainly as his Orestes stands for freedom of action and human dignity. Her traditional role of waiting for Orestes to come and avenge her is therefore stressed right at the outset. She says to Orestes, who is going under the name of Philebes : "Someone else will come and set me free. My brother isn't dead, I know. . . . I must stay here to guide his rage. . .to point at the guilty and say : There they are, Orestes. Strike !" (*The Flies*, p. 64). Even so, Electra's inciting to murder is not so strongly stressed in Sartre as, say, in Sophocles. She does not really dare to carry out her desires. In a very natural reaction, her desire to see the deed done is mixed with fear of it : "You have come after all, Orestes, and your mind is made up. And here am I, just as I am in my dreams, standing on the brink of an irreparable act, and I am afraid, just as I am in my dreams. Oh, how long I have waited for this moment—and dreaded it !" (p. 73).

What does this mean in the context of Sartre's philosophy? It means that Electra does not choose her deed, that, unlike Orestes, she does not want to be answerable for her will and her actions. It is also characteristic that her motives are quite different from those of Orestes. In earlier interpretations brother and sister are inspired by the same motive and are of one mind in the execution of the murder. In Sartre, however, their basic situations are entirely different. Electra hates her mother for natural reasons : as the murderer of her father and because she herself is forced to lead a miserable life in Clytemnestra's house. Orestes, as we have seen, acts out of idealistic, not personal, motives : for the sake of freedom and man's human dignity. Thus Sartre completely reverses the traditional relationship of the pair toward each other and toward the deed. In the Greek tragedies Electra is the strong, resolute one on whom Orestes leans; in Sartre, by contrast, she is weak, despairing, seeking protection from the Furies. It is she, not Orestes, who sees them : "Orestes! There they are! Where have they come from?" Orestes, seeing only ordinary flies, answers indifferently, "What do the flies matter to us?" But Electra recognizes them as goddesses of vengeance : "Listen! Listen to the sound of their wings. . . .They're all around us, Orestes. They're watching us. Presently they'll swarm down upon us. . . .We'll never escape them" (p. 92).

The final scene is then skillfully brought to its climax, like a philosophical argument. Electra is forced to choose between Orestes and Jupiter, that is, between guilt and remorse. For guilt is Orestes' portion and at the same time, as we have seen, his freedom. Remorse, however, is the ransom payable to Jupiter for deliverance from guilt. From remorse Jupiter derives his power over men, giving them absolution in return. Here the notion of freedom appears in its dual sense. Absolution, deliverance from guilt by the grace of God at the price of "a little bit of remorse"—this is Electra's nonfreedom. "Take care, Electra," begs Orestes. "That mere nothing will weigh like a mountain on your soul." Jupiter tries to persuade her that she never willed or desired the crime : "Why hesitate to disavow that crime? It was somebody else who committed it; you could hardly even be called his accomplice. . . .You never willed to do evil. . . .At an age when children are still playing with dolls. . . you played at murder." Orestes beseeches her not to deny that she willed it : "Electra! Electra! It's *now* you are guilty. Who can know what you really wanted except you yourself? Will you let someone else decide that for you?" (pp. 107–108). Unheeding, Electra throws herself at Jupiter's feet. The flies leave her. But she is not a human being in Sartre's sense. She does not choose her deed, her guilt, her willing, her "act," her autonomous actions; hence she does not choose herself, does not posit herself as a free human being, does not assume responsibility for herself.

The significance of responsibility in Sartre's activistic theory of freedom is revealed even more clearly in the comparatively simple negative case of Electra than in the positive but more complicated case of Orestes. The term "responsibility" as we use it today implies that one should be responsible for other people besides oneself, not in the sense of taking charge of them but by serving as an exemplary model, even as their representative. When I posit myself as a free man, answerable for myself, I do it on behalf of all mankind. "In saying that man is responsible for himself, we do not mean that he merely wishes to be responsible for his own individuality but that he is responsible for all men," says Sartre in *L'existentialisme est un humanisme* (p. 25). In contrast to Orestes' extreme responsibility and freedom, Electra, who does not even want to be responsible for herself, acts irresponsibly in the true sense of the word.

If Giraudoux's *Electre* had not appeared in 1937, six years before *The Flies,* it might almost be taken for an answer to Sartre's play. Here Electra is condemned for reasons which are the exact opposite of Sartre's. In Giraudoux too Electra behaves irresponsibly. Here, however, this does not mean what it means according to Sartre's activistic theory of freedom : that she is unwilling to take responsibility for what she wants and thus deprives herself of human dignity. Here irresponsibility implies a wrong toward others, which is what we generally mean when we say that somebody is acting irresponsibly. In what way does Giraudoux see and condemn Electra's conduct as irresponsible? This emerges only when we explore the view of life that pervades this play, a view which in fact offers the greatest conceivable contrast to Sartre's.

Unlike Sartre, Giraudoux is neither a moralist nor an existentialist. He is not concerned with the showing man makes as man; what interests him is how he copes with life and circumstances as they are. He would never require, as Sartre does, that once thrown into the world, man is to be held responsible for everything he does. The essential thing in man's life, be he king or beggar, is the present, the here and now, the actuality of daily life and its demands. In his remarkable play, whose setting hovers even more indeterminately than that of *The Flies* between Greek antiquity and the present day, Giraudoux presents an Argos quite different from and, one might say, more serene than the one in the classical *Oresteia* and in Sartre.

The situation in this city and in the palace of the Atridae is this : Agamemnon is dead, said—and generally believed—to have slipped on the tiles surrounding the bath. Clytemnestra and Aegisthus are there, in this case not even married yet; in any case, they are ruling Argos and are for the time being the recognized regents. This Clytemnestra can quite credibly claim to be happy in her love for Aegisthus and with the inner justification of genuine love can refute Electra's reproach of having "taken a lover." What happened in the past—the murder of her husband, the adultery—belongs to the past, no longer exists, has no relevance, no validity, no reality any more. Ideas such as justice, law, tradition, blood vengeance, divine command are ideas and nothing more, devoid of reality and existence; they become dangerous or troublesome only when people insist on putting them into practice, because then they disrupt life. As Theocathocles, the chief justice (one of the characters whom Giraudoux added to the traditional cast), says : "Justice, generosity, and duty, not selfishness and cleverness, are what ruin the state, the individual and the best families."[3]

In the reality of their daily life and needs, people do not live with lofty emotions and ideas, and thus the somber, bloody story of the House of Atreus is drained of its high tragedy, given a tone of irony, reduced in scale. The monstrous crime is made trifling. Clytemnestra openly admits that she hates Agamemnon. Even to call it hatred is too much : she simply cannot stand him; she has an aversion to him. Why? He always had an irritating way of crooking his little finger, which was as obnoxious to her as his carefully curled golden hair. When she calls to mind the sacrifice of Iphigenia it is not the terrible event itself that dominates her memory and feelings, but the way Agamemnon crooked his little finger even on that occasion. "From the day he appeared with his curled beard to take me away from home, with that hand of his with the little finger always sticking out, I hated him. He crooked it in drinking; he crooked it when he was driving and his horse bolted, in holding his sceptre. . . and when he put your sister Iphigenia to death at dawn—my god, I saw the little finger of both hands silhouetted against the sun !" (p. 104). Great passions are reduced to a commonplace erotic aversion which, according to this view of life, is sufficient motive for murdering one's husband. On the other hand, in this climate of skeptical, non-tragic rationalism, the characters are also humanized by not being treated in the exalted style of high tragedy. Aegisthus and Clytemnestra, both murderers, are thoroughly likable people to whose reasonable views no one could take exception; the people of Argos are content under their enlightened rule.

The principle behind Giraudoux's treatment of the theme is to reduce it to the scale of human life. Life is all that matters. But life is disrupted if past crimes are kept alive by hatred and revenge. Even if Agamemnon was murdered, what good will revenge do anybody? What good does justice do anybody, or the right to revenge, or expiation? Chief Justice Theocathocles, who concurs in this attitude with his lord and master Aegisthus, says : "The only element . . .really fatal to humanity is embittered tenacity." The word "humanity" means both the human race as a whole and humanness, so that this key term in Giraudoux's *Electre* also conveys the ethical idea that embittered insistence upon a right, however legitimate it may be, is ultimately inhuman. This is stated again and again. The gardener whom Electra is supposed to marry says : "Joy and love . . .are preferable to bitterness and hatred. . . .Of course life's a mess, but it's good, life is, very good" (p. 59). And even one of the "little Eumenides," that is to say, the goddess of vengeance herself, utters the warning : "The righters of wrongs are the curse of the world."

It is already clear how Electra is conceived in this play, against the background of this amoral philosophy of life. She is a disturbing element in the kingdom of Aegisthus and Clytemnestra because she stands for the hating, anti-life principle. Giraudoux deviates from the traditional legend in order to transform the clearly defined, well-known story of Electra into a principle, to present it as a classic example of one of the disruptions that mar men's lives. Here Electra knows nothing of her mother's crime. Giraudoux deliberately takes some ten years off her age at the time of Agamemnon's murder to make her a child when it occurred. Neither does she know that Aegisthus is her mother's lover, so that the fact that they are not married, insignificant and hardly meaningful in itself, nevertheless supports the contextual idea of the play. The crime itself is secondary; the primary thing is the mental climate of hatred and bitterness which is inimical to happiness in life (represented by the gardener and by Orestes). Even though there are indications that Electra suspects and always has suspected what happened long ago, even though she does intuitively learn the truth through a vision of her father in a dream, a straightforward explanation of this kind is not incorporated in the structure of meaning.

The concept of "the little Eumenides," one of the major changes and innovations that Giraudoux made in the traditional story, argues against any such explanation. Whenever the Furies appear in any Oresteia from Greek antiquity down to our own time, they appear as goddesses of vengeance, relentlessly seeking out their victim. In Giraudoux, on the contrary, they are beings who do all they can to prevent the man charged with matricide from killing his mother. They are Electra's inseparable companions : personifications of her inborn hatred. Little girls when the play opens, they grow with Electra's hatred, until in the end, after Clytemnestra has been killed, they are the same size and age as Electra herself. But they are recalcitrant personifications of Electra's hatred. As goddesses of vengeance they do not amount to very much. Good little harmless spirits, Eumenides as Aeschylus conceived them in the third play of his *Oresteia,* they stand on the side of humanity, for forgiving and forgetting, for life, seconding Aegisthus and the chief justice. Their warnings against hatred and revenge make the crime which calls for revenge less weighty than hatred in the totality of life and world order. "Look at the two innocents. The fruit of their marriage [the reunion of Electra and Orestes] will be to restore to life for the world and for the ages a crime which is already done with. And its expiation will be an even worse crime" (p. 57), says the beggar, a mysterious figure who is obviously a god, a Jupiter in disguise.

Only Electra's hatred—and this is the other change Giraudoux has made—brings to light and gives reality to the crime committed and even concealed so long ago, a crime which is for this very reason harmless. Aegisthus says that this hate-filled Electra is the only person who still gives signs to the gods—a reversal of the ancient belief that the gods gave signs to men, as Apollo did through his oracles, and in this way often led them into misfortune. "Every evening she goes and lures back everything which but for her would have abandoned this land of easy-going pleasure : the remorse, the confessions, the old bloodstains, the rust, the bones of the victims of murder, the rubble of tale-bearing" (p. 17)—things which are not to be taken in their literal sense but are cited as symbols of the general mood of hatred and bitterness. This is why Aegisthus wants to get rid of Electra and render her harmless by marrying her to the gardener, who, of course (tending, cultivating, and loving natural things), represents the principle of sheer love of life to which Electra can never surrender. Through Orestes (who again appears as a stranger before making his identity known), another innocent, life-accepting, life-loving man, she obtains her "justice" after all and in obtaining it is branded as guilty and irresponsible. She sacrifices the beleaguered city to her lust for revenge, inasmuch as her preoccupation with her discovery of the murder prevents Aegisthus from defending it. She obtains her justice and her truth; Orestes kills his mother, and the Eumenides are forced to descend upon him. In Electra's guise they will pursue him until, despairing of himself, he takes his own life and curses his sister. When Electra insists that she has nonetheless triumphed, has achieved justice and a clear conscience, this too is carried *ad absurdum*. "Your conscience! You'll hear from your conscience in the early mornings that lie ahead of you. For seven years you couldn't sleep because of a crime committed by other people. From now on you are the guilty one" (p. 112).

Here Hans Rothe's German translation of *Electre* retains a passage from an earlier, unpublished version of the play which is worth quoting because it again contrasts very strikingly the right of life with the sterile idea of abstract justice. One of the Eumenides says to Electra : "Take a look at your justice. Weigh it in your innocent hands and tell me how many fish it will get you on the shore, how many loaves of bread at the baker's shop. A lot of good your justice does you! From today on it's not worth a dead crow."[4]

It is surprising and at the same time very illuminating to discover the quite separate, antithetical directions taken by French dramatists of the last three decades in dealing with the Electra problem. What is accentuated to the extreme in Sartre—man's freedom of choice and his responsibility for his freedom—is to Giraudoux uninteresting, devoid of validity, even threatening. For Giraudoux the moral imperative, right, duty, and so-called justice are hubris, man's hubris in the face of the greater power of life. The tragedy of the House of Atreus—that blood vengeance can breed only more blood vengeance, a fact which the chorus deplores even in Aeschylus—serves in Giraudoux as an exemplary warning against disrupting life through law and justice. The final words of Schiller's *The Bride of Messina,* the play in which he tried to revive Greek tragedy, say that life is not the highest good of all, but guilt is the greatest of evils. Giraudoux's *Electra* might almost be an attack upon this high-flown ethic of human dignity, which reaches its climax in Sartre, upon this classical idea of morality. It is no accident that this *Electra* dissolves the form of high tragedy in irony. The exact opposite of Schiller's lines would apply to this play : life is the highest good of all; he who avenges evil is the curse of the world.

Giraudoux's conception of the Electra problem is undoubtedly just as novel and untraditional as Sartre's antithetical one. Nevertheless we can find a germ of this conception in Greek antiquity, not yet in Aeschylus' prototypal Electra, but in the characterization of the figure as seen by Sophocles, the first dramatist to devote a whole play in his *Oresteia* to Electra. His play establishes her as a woman totally consumed by lust for revenge, but also as one who suffers. The germ of Giraudoux's theme of sinning against life lies in a figure introduced by Sophocles who has not hitherto played a part, either in the legend or in Aeschylus : Chrysothemis, third daughter of the House of Atreus. It is she who stands for the principle of forgiveness, worldly wisdom, acceptance of things as they are, in contrast to her fanatically uncompromising sister :

> What have you come to say out of doors,
> sister? Will you never learn, in all this time,
> not to give way to your empty anger?
> Yet this much I know, and know my own heart, too,
> that I am sick at what I see, so that
> if I had strength, I would let them know how I feel.
> But under pain of punishment, I think,
> I must make my voyage with lowered sails,
> that I may not seem to do something and then prove
> ineffectual.   (Sophocles, p. 138)

The Chrysothemis in Hofmannsthal's *Elektra* reiterates :

> Have pity on us both. Who benefits
> from all this agony? Our father?
> Our father's dead. Our brother stays away.   (p. 19)

The will-for-life motif is even more strongly accentuated in Hofmannsthal's Chrysothemis than in Sophocles', and this is characteristic since the modern writer profiles his characters more sharply and more deliberately than the classical one—a process which our present thesis shows up very clearly. Hofmannsthal's Chrysothemis complains of her lot, for which her embittered sister is to blame. She is confined at home, constantly watched :

> It's you who keep me welded to the floor
> with iron bolts. If it were not for you
> they'd let us out!
> I must get out! I can't sleep here
> night after night until I die! I want to live
> before I die! I want to bear a child
> before my body shrivels.   (p. 18)

Her protestation that what is truly disastrous for mankind is bitterness comes close to Giraudoux's theme :

> The heart of man was never meant to bear
> that horror! When that threatens,
> he ought to leave his house, escape outdoors
> into the vineyards, up into the hills . . . .
> Never remain with it. Never stay
> under one roof with that!   (p. 21)

But it only comes close to it; for Hofmannsthal this never becomes the crucial, sustaining theme. In Sophocles and in Hofmannsthal, Chrysothemis, the upholder of the right to life against the destructive right to revenge, is not the one who triumphs or pronounces the sentence; it is Electra who wins the moral victory over her more cowardly, compromising sister. In Sophocles the chorus sings her praises as having rejected dishonor "to win at once two reputations/as wise and best of daughters" (p. 167).

But in Hofmannsthal's modern version—and again this is characteristic—Electra's victory is not quite so clear-cut; at any rate something is left open. "Electra's relation to the deed treated with irony, though," Hofmannsthal writes in the notes. He adds, "*Ad me ipsum.*"[5] The restrictive "though" refers to the anything but ironical motive of loyalty which inspires Electra's whole life, her actions, and her determination to commit the act of matricide. Hofmannsthal also noted that this loyalty motive was developed to the extreme in *Elektra* (p. 221). In Sophocles' *Electra*, filial affection and loyalty toward her murdered father are already inextricably mixed with hatred of her mother. But Hofmannsthal underlines the loyalty, of which revengefulness and the refusal to forget are an intrinsic part, underlines her inability to forget and hence her inability to live, her constant reliving of past events, the attitude that nothing is "over," with which Chrysothemis reproaches her :

> Over? In there it's all begun again!
> Don't think that I don't recognize the sound
> a corpse makes as they drag it down the stairs.
> The whispering. The blood-soaked cloths wrung out.   (p. 22)

Yet the motive of loyalty carried to the extreme is still not completely unproblematical and absolute. Filial loyalty which demands the murder of one's mother is a questionable loyalty fraught with irony in the most sublime sense. Certainly the irony is not immediately obvious in the text or the handling of the plot, but it is nonetheless concealed in the inner impossibility of Electra's tragic situation. It shows itself in the figure of Chrysothemis, whose natural will for life almost gets the better of Electra's will for revenge and murder. But this conflict and contrast grows even more acute and becomes for the first time truly ironical in the meeting between Clytemnestra and Electra. For here this murderer actually seems to be to some extent in the right against Electra. Hofmannsthal produces this effect by suggesting the tormented, desperate mental state of this woman who long ago acted in response to a half-unconscious instinct and is now ready to live and let live. She too speaks of forgetting, of the changes life brings :

> For does not everything dissolve and shift
> like mist before our eyes? And we ourselves!
> And our deeds! Deeds! We and deeds!
> What do words mean? Am I then *still*
> the woman who performed that deed? And if I am?
> Done! Done!   (p. 35)

But Electra's overwrought, ecstatic triumph, which collapses just as it reaches its climax, makes one ask whether there is not something unresolved, something uncertain in her absoluteness, even if it is the absoluteness of loyalty. While the murder of the king and queen arouses frenzied rejoicing in Chrysothemis and the courtiers, Electra in her ecstasy goes into a maenadic dance :

> Be silent now and dance. Come. All must join in.
> Bearing my load of happiness I dance
> in front of all of you.
> Whoever shares our happiness must do just that:
> dance and be silent.   (p. 75)

Dancing, she collapses; the curtain falls upon her rigid body. The final stage direction says simply : "Silence." It is the silence of death. It is quite logical and in accordance with the modern sense of tragedy that, contrary to tradition, Electra should not survive her triumph, that her story should not have a happy ending. Besides, Hofmannsthal's highly developed sense of style could never have permitted such a fundamentally tragic figure, whose tragedy he had heightened even further, to remain alive, untragically. But apart from this, Electra's death and the word "silence" can be interpreted as the open question whether Electra, a human being, a girl, has not, as it were, overreached her humanity and her maidenhood, has not gone too far, thus even anticipating Giraudoux's problem : whether men are called upon at all to exact vengeance and in doing so to violate life.[6]

That is still not the end of the Electra theme in world drama. Sartre focused attention on Electra's share in the deed, her responsibility, and the problem of her guilt, but other aspects of this classical figure have also challenged dramatists to make it a vehicle for modern themes. The path that leads from Aeschylus and Sophocles to O'Neill follows different motifs from the path leading to Sartre and Giraudoux. One might in fact say that the conception of Electra that finally culminates in O'Neill's play is much more obvious, much more traditional, than that of Sartre and Giraudoux, which first brought to light an intrinsic but concealed element in this figure. This element is not the primary reason why dramatic interest has focused on Electra in preference to Orestes. Rather, her particular individuality has caused her to come to the fore whenever the dramatist's interest in people was psychological rather than philosophical or ethical. This was first the case with Sophocles, and a survey of the extant work of this tragedian will show that it was not by chance that he made Electra and not Orestes the central figure.

Of the three tragedians Sophocles is the one who saw his characters from the standpoint of human greatness. All his heroes attain monumental stature, more or less irrespective of their motivation, since this is an absolute greatness. The motive may be trivial and apparently out of proportion to the suffering and destruction, as it is in the case of the mad Ajax, who suffers terrible shame, from which only death offers an escape, because, led astray by Athena in the darkness, he has slaughtered cattle instead of heroes. The only thing that matters is that man dedicate himself uncompromisingly and entirely, that he sacrifice himself to what he himself sees as the right, the essential, no matter what suffering, even including death, he may risk. Oedipus, innocent of what he has committed, still takes the consequences entirely upon himself and does not try to blame the oracle, chance, his unwitting innocence. On penalty of death Antigone buries her brother in defiance of Creon's prohibition. Human greatness arises out of suffering, so that suffering and greatness merge.[7]

Electra too could be conceived along these lines. We need only to compare Sophocles' Electra with those of Aeschylus and Euripides to see how Sophocles made her the embodiment of suffering and greatness purified of all the extraneous and fortuitous elements of the legend. It is true that she does not perish; she does not pay the price of death. But neither is she concerned with her personal future and happiness, as she is in Aeschylus; nor does her story end happily with her betrothal to Pylades, as it does in Euripides and almost all the later versions down to Gerhart Hauptmann's House of Atreus tetralogy. There is no Pylades in Sophocles' play; Sophocles replaced Orestes' companion, probably deliberately, in line with his conception of Electra, by a tutor. Thus when Hofmannsthal's Electra, who is a free adaptation of Sophocles', collapses in her wild maenadic dance, when the play ends in death and "silence," this is a logical ending for the Sophoclean conception. In Sophocles, Electra's last speech expresses only satisfaction that retribution is about to overtake Aegisthus too. Now that Clytemnestra is dead, she urges that it be exacted :

> Kill him as quickly as you can. And killing
> throw him out to find such burial as suits him
> out of our sights. This is the only thing
> than can bring me redemption from
> all my past sufferings.   (p. 186)

It was Sophocles who established the conception of Electra that has remained dominant : the woman who hates fanatically and who suffers, and it was he who endowed her with the psychological traits necessary for this : purity and passion—passion arising out of the profundity of her emotional nature, which expresses itself, which in fact totally concentrates and expends itself, in love for her murdered father :

> . . .never shall I give over my sorrow,
> and the number of my dirges none shall tell. . . .
> What is the natural measure of my sorrow?
> Come, how when the dead are in question,
> can it be honorable to forget?
> In what human being is this instinctive?
> Never may I have honor of such,
> nor, if I dwell with any good thing,
> may I live at ease, by restraining
> the wings of shrill lament to my father's dishonor.   (pp. 134–135)

Strong in love and hatred, "a wild, fiery soul," as Goethe called her—such is the Sophoclean Electra. But interfused with this is a rigorous chastity, her second basic character trait, which offers the first plausible explanation—and a brilliant one—for the hatred and loathing she feels for her adulterous mother :

> —if mother I should call her,
> this woman that sleeps with him.
> She is so daring that she paramours
> this foul, polluted creature and fears no Fury.   (p. 136)

Again Hofmannsthal develops this motif even more strongly; his Electra is created out of twin flames of hatred and chastity. The chastity motif is suggested in such splendid lines as these :

> I think that I was lovely. When I blew out
> the lamp before my glass I used to feel
> with a chaste shudder how my naked form,
> untouched in its virginity, shone forth
> godlike into the sultry night.   (p. 62)

In the extreme ecstatic quality of Hofmannsthal's Electra, however, the notion of chastity is almost dialectically reversed into the completely negative, utterly unreal and visionary realization of

her womanhood, to which her suffering and hatred bring her.
Impregnated with the hatred which her dead father has "sent her
as a bridegroom" instead of the natural love of a maid for a man,
she matures into a woman who is and can be nothing but an
avenger—vengeance personified :

> I had to let that hateful man
> into my sleepless bed. His viper's breath
> on top of me, forcing me to learn
> everything that a man and woman do!
> Oh, those nights in which I came to know it!
> My body cold as ice, yet charred and burned
> inside. And when at last I knew it all,
> then I was wise. And then the murderers—
> I mean my mother and that man of hers—
> no longer dared to meet my eye.   (p. 63)

This passage occurs shortly after the one quoted above suggesting the chastity motif—a dubious chastity, to be sure. We called the
sudden change from Electra's chastity to the experience of "love"
dialectical, but this passage in fact takes on a dialectical significance
in the Electra theme as a whole—as well as in general. What is here
expressed suggestively rather than directly is a synthesis taking
shape out of the antitheses of chastity and passion and forming the
complex Electra figure which is finally presented in O'Neill as a
generalized "Electra complex."

Here, however, another factor arises, one of decisive importance
for the thematic problem : Electra's relationship to Clytemnestra.
It is extremely interesting to see how the psychological deepening of
Electra, what we might call the existential conception of this character as against the ideological conception of Sartre and Giraudoux
(though Giraudoux's Electra really stands midway between the two),
brings her into an increasingly strong relationship with Clytemnestra
and how it becomes plain that mother and daughter are much more
closely akin than the traditional story reveals. They are akin and
yet different : two elemental, passionate, uncontrolled women who
repel each other according to the law of equally charged poles. Even
Aeschylus seems already to have perceived and subtly suggested
this. Electra's prayer to Hermes and her father hints that she senses
the danger in the closeness of their natures :

> And for myself, grant that I be more temperate
> of heart than my mother; that I act with purer hand.
>
> *(Libation Bearers,* p. 140)

Thus, once again, the modern writers are expressing something which for the Greeks cannot yet be a real psychological problem differentiated to this extent but can be, at most, implicitly indicated. Hofmannsthal's Orestes puts it quite plainly when he asks : "Sister, is not our mother much like you?" (p. 65). The kinship is more realistically, not to say cynically, shown in Giraudoux. Here, however, because of the nature of the play as a whole, it is perhaps too consciously stressed as a motive by both Clytemnestra and Electra. Here Clytemnestra accuses her daughter of exactly the uninhibited eroticism that is traditionally part of her own character, although she here disclaims it. She seems to see through Electra's much vaunted chastity : "Chastity ! This girl devoured by her desires speaks to us of chastity ! This girl who at the age of two couldn't look at a boy without blushing" (p. 44).

In all these cases, however, these traits are secondary, not central, characteristics. They are thus symptomatic of the changes the Electra concept has undergone and of the development of germs already existing in the antique versions. We should scarcely need to touch upon them if it were not for O'Neill's great work *Mourning Becomes Electra,* which stands out in modern world drama with a certain monumentality.

As we know, O'Neill freed himself from the historical facts of the Atridae theme. *Mourning Becomes Electra* is a family tragedy in a small New England town in the 1860's—the tragedy of the Mannons. At the same time it is of course a deliberate transposition of the legend of the House of Atreus into modern times. The symbolic use in the title of the name Electra for a heroine who in the play is called Lavinia or Vinnie, and of the name Orin, with its obvious echoes of Orestes, for her younger brother, reveals O'Neill's intention to show that the ancient tragedy can repeat itself among human beings of the bourgeois nineteenth century and to attest its universal human significance. The form too announces his intention. *Mourning Becomes Electra* is a trilogy modeled on the *Oresteia* of Aeschylus, except that the third play does not bring expiation. The stage setting also deliberately recalls that of the Greek tragedies. The Mannon house, the stage directions say, is a large Greek-revival mansion, and most of the action takes place in front of the white columned portico, much as the action in the Greek theater did. The antique archetypes on which the characters are modeled are clearly discernible; they, not the plot, are the essential thing. The action, though basically modeled on the classical story, follows it very loosely.

The father, General Ezra Mannon, who has returned home from the Civil War on the day the play begins, is of course the Agamemnon. His wife, Christine, is the Clytemnestra; Lavinia and Orin represent Electra and Orestes. There is an Aegisthus figure too : Christine's lover, a Captain Brant, who, like the Greek Aegisthus, is related to the family but out of hatred for Ezra Mannon (the reasons for which we need not go into here) has changed his name. The husband is killed by poison which Brant provides at Christine's instigation. The second play, *The Hunted*, deals with the revenge of the brother and sister (essentially, Lavinia's, however). They murder Captain Brant on his ship. There is, however, no actual matricide : after Brant's death Christine Mannon commits suicide. Nonetheless Orin, who is very close to his beautiful mother, blames himself for her death and thus sees himself guilty of matricide, and he too takes his own life. Lavinia, who for a time had intended to marry her young cousin, is left behind, the prey to terrible anguish—the title of the third play is *The Haunted*—tormented by the spirits of the dead, pursued by the evil destiny of the House of Atreus. The play ends with her immuring herself in the gloomy house, whose shutters are nailed closed forever. There can be no expiation such as we find in the original *Oresteia*.

There can be no expiation and no reconciliation because in this play destiny is no longer fulfilled through external circumstances but through the particular nature of the characters—with which it is in fact identical. Only the two women, the mother and daughter, are important; the other characters are not decisive but merely serve the purposes of the action. But the mother-daughter relationship, already touched upon in the Greek tragedies, becomes truly thematic for the first time in O'Neill.

Mourning Becomes Electra appeared in 1931, when Freudian psychoanalysis was being widely discussed and was influencing both the writing and the interpretation of literature. With some justification it has been taken as a typical dramatization of the psycho-

analytical incest problem, of the Electra complex, as Freud named
the counterpart of the better-known and psychoanalytically more
important Oedipus complex. Freud interpreted the Oedipus legend
as a mythological symbolization of the son's infantile mother fixation, which arouses his unconscious wish to kill his father-rival and
marry his mother. Similarly the Electra situation represents the
daughter's father fixation, which leads her to identify herself with
her mother, to want to take her mother's place with her father, and
therefore to hate her mother.[8] We do not need to go into the infantile sexual and biological phenomena on which Freud based these
complexes, since only the result, the adult's relationship to his
mother or father, is relevant to the literary application of Freud's
incest theory.

Assuming that we accept the Freudian interpretation of the
legends, it seems more plausible to relate the Oedipus story than the
Electra story to unconscious psychic processes. Oedipus unknowingly
kills his father and marries his mother. Unknowingly does not of
course mean the same as unconsciously. But, as Freud says, "the
ignorance of Oedipus is a legitimate representation of the uncon-
sciousness into which, for adults, the whole experience has fallen."[9]
The crucial element of unknowingness is not found in the Electra
legend; there is nothing but a completely conscious wish, a
resolutely pursued determination, to kill her mother, together with
a love for her father (already emphasized by the classical tragedians)
which adds emotional depth to her desire to see Orestes exact blood
vengeance. In Euripides' *Electra* Clytemnestra herself brings this
home to her daughter, and the motive is thus given more promi-
nence than if it were suggested by Electra's words alone :

> My child, from birth you always have adored your father.
> This is part of life. Some children always love
> the male, some turn more closely to their mother than him.
> I know you and forgive you.   (p. 55)

Unlike the Oedipus story, the Electra legend and the Greek
tragedians' interpretations of it contain neither the factor of unknowingness nor the committing of incest, and this seems to explain
why Electra's psychological state and Freud's Electra complex have
been more challenging to modern dramatists than the Oedipus complex or the Oedipus figure in general. That which has not been

enacted but has merely been felt or desired is a matter of latent possibility rather than fact, and so offers more scope for literary creativity. Electra's desire to kill her mother could be attributed to a father fixation, even though any incestuous action was precluded by the legend. Her real—and traditional—motive in urging the killing of her mother in revenge for Clytemnestra's murder of her husband would then be exposed as a masking of her unconscious incestuous desires, or even, more consciously, as a screen which allows Electra to deceive herself.

There is no doubt that O'Neill does make use of the Electra complex. In the first scene between the mother and daughter, Christine tells Electra-Lavinia to her face : "I know you, Vinnie. I've watched you ever since you were little, trying to do exactly what you're doing now. You've tried to become the wife of your father and the mother of Orin! You've always schemed to steal my place."[10] Indeed, O'Neill stresses Lavinia's passionate love for her father, as revealed in the homecoming scene, for instance, as well as her jealousy of Orin, their mother's favorite, and, even more, her jealousy of Brant, her mother's lover. There is no doubt that Electra's desire to get rid of her mother and take her place pervades her relationship with all three men.

Yet to interpret O'Neill's *Mourning Becomes Electra* purely as a manifestation of an incestuous Electra complex seems inadequate. The dramatic, or rather psychological, conflict on which it is based is a wider one. Here the traditional Clytemnestra-Electra relationship is sharpened to culminate in a clash between two sensual women of the same type whose passions are no less ardent for being somber. They are closely akin and therefore they repel one another to the point of mutual destruction. O'Neill made this very clear in the expansive, descriptively written stage directions which are so characteristic of him. He keeps reverting to the outward resemblance and equally marked differences between the two women. When Lavinia comes out on to the steps of the house, where Christine has just been standing, her mother is described as a fine, voluptuous figure, who moves with a flowing animal grace. She has thick copper-bronze hair and dark violet, deep-set eyes. The stage directions then describe Lavinia : "Tall like her mother, her body is thin, flat-breasted and angular, and its unattractiveness is accentuated by her plain black dress. Her movements are stiff and she

carries herself with a wooden, square-shouldered, military bearing
. . . .but in spite of these dissimilarities one is immediately struck by
her facial resemblance to her mother. She has the same. . .copper-
gold hair. . .and dark violet-blue eyes" (pp. 21–23).

Obviously it is difficult to make this ambivalent similarity and
dissimilarity visible on the stage, in the actresses. O'Neill is a very
epic dramatist, who seeks to transcend the limit imposed by the
genre upon the description of environment and physical detail by
means of extensive stage directions going far beyond the normal
range. While he continually emphasizes Lavinia's puritanically aus-
tere appearance, her thinness, her black, nunlike dress, his extension
of the stage directions to include even psychic traits shows that her
appearance is not meant to denote a genuinely chaste, nunlike mode
of existence but a life of duress, of being forced to forgo all that her
mother enjoys as a sensually attractive, beautiful, radiant woman
who wins the love of men. Hofmannsthal had already adumbrated
the elements of chastity inherent in the Electra figure as the obverse
of an erotic, libidinous element. In O'Neill it emerges perfectly
plainly as being nothing but the forcible repression of the erotic
instinct that makes Electra her mother's daughter. The daughter
shares her mother's nature, but in her it is oriented toward the dark
side of life. The fact that Lavinia loves all the men who love her
mother (her father, her brother and—though this, of course, she
barely admits to herself—the insignificant Brant) seems to have less
to do with the Electra incest complex than with their similarity in
nature and character. However, this distinction cannot be made
with any precision because the one is manifested through the other
and, to push the matter farther, because instinctual psychic processes cannot be broken down into separate, explicable elements.
This is the realm of the sub-rational, the irrational. Lavinia acts in
response to her deeply confused, instinctive nature, which is far less
able to understand itself, far less aware of itself, than is the case with
her mother. After Christine kills her husband, this Electra resolves
to kill not her mother but Brant, the Aegisthus figure. Certainly the
action is directed against her mother, but evidently her deeper, unconscious motive is to revenge herself on the man she loves, who
loves her mother instead of herself.

When both Brant and her mother are dead, Lavinia blossoms in
a remarkable way, for she now has in her power the one survivor

of the men her mother possessed, her brother Orin, whom she makes completely subservient to her. For once she has succeeded in taking her mother's place, and now the stage directions describe how she assumes her mother's outward appearance, dresses like her, takes on her mature, attractive femininity, until she becomes the image of Christine and at first glance might even be mistaken for her. She blossoms; she wins the love of her cousin Peter and becomes engaged to be married to him, until the man she thinks she possesses, Orin, eludes her through his own death. But the curse upon the house continues to work through the dead Orin, destroying all hope of redemption through pure love, such as might have emerged from Lavinia's association with the young Peter. Orin, who hates his sister because of the murder they have committed and who demands atonement, leaves a note for the engaged couple in which he accuses Lavinia, rightly or wrongly, of having lost her virginity. Whether this twist in the story is successful or not is irrelevant; the point here —and this is what distinguishes the Mannon family tragedy from the legend of the Atridae on which it is based—is that everything that happens—murder, guilt, and suffering—is relegated to the dark realm of the instincts instead of being somehow brought up into the consciousness where a healing process could ensue.

Wolfgang Schadewaldt said of Sophocles' *Electra* that the matricide, and hence Electra's determination to act, represent "the cleansing, through the sacrifice of suffering in accordance with the will of the gods, of a world utterly corrupted by the murder of Agamemnon."[11] The exact opposite is true of O'Neill's Electra: hers is a godless world in which man and his actions no longer have any connection with divine will and man is thrown back upon himself. This may come about in the way in which Sartre understands the notion of man thrown back upon himself: as the humanistic freedom and responsibility of the man who no longer needs God. But it may also mean the abandonment of man to his instincts, which is the fate of O'Neill's characters—and not only those in *Mourning Becomes Electra*. Lavinia Mannon's suffering represents not a cleansing but a confirmation of the corruption of the world and thus of the inevitability of suffering itself, from which even bodily death cannot offer deliverance—as it still can to Hofmannsthal's Electra. Lavinia imprisons herself in her house for the rest of a long life to atone for the curse of the sensuality which has destroyed her race and which will not be wiped out until "the last Mannon is let die."

There is no doubt that from Electra's character as the Greek tragedians had already formulated it, even such an ultimately nihilistic conclusion could be drawn—as it has been drawn by writers of our time and world for whom, behind humanism as European classicism had understood it, there came into view again the dark, chthonian, instinct-dominated ground from which new threats to humanity can always arise again. Gerhart Hauptmann's conception of Iphigenia bears this out in quite a different way from O'Neill's Electra play and on a broader scale—in a more unexpected way too, since the noble figure of Iphigenia, as literature has conceived it, seems much less apt than the passionate Electra to become connected with chthonian forces of this kind.

ᘒ 4 ᘒ

IPHIGENIA

The story of Iphigenia, eldest daughter of Agamemnon and Clytemnestra, occupies a special place in the saga of the House of Atreus and its dramatic interpretations. From the viewpoint of myth in literature and the evolution of the problem, it stands completely apart from the *Oresteia*, although it is associated with that work as an important part of its prehistory and also by the fact that Orestes (and in Gerhart Hauptmann, Electra too) appears in the Iphigenia plays. Another indication of its special place is that there are fewer Iphigenia plays in world literature than plays about Orestes and Electra, especially in modern literature, where only one writer, Gerhart Hauptmann, has attempted this subject. Seeking the reason for this, we may come to the purely hypothetical conclusion that the problem of Iphigenia seemed less challenging to the dramatists than the problem of her younger sister. Iphigenia was a victim, sacrificed at Aulis, whereas Orestes and Electra are active characters; as we have tried to show, their situation offered the dramatists a many-faceted complex of problems. Iphigenia, on the other hand, provided almost no basis for a conflict of conscience or action. Only her tragic and unusual mythical history was of any interest. Thus only three important versions of the Iphigenia story exist : those of Euripides, Goethe, and Hauptmann.

Another factor that makes this legend a special case is that it falls into two parts, each presenting separate problems : Iphigenia at Aulis, the story of her sacrifice; and Iphigenia in Tauris, the story of how she became a priestess of Artemis and escaped back to Greece with Orestes and Pylades. Plays by Euripides exist on both subjects; Goethe wrote only an Iphigenia in Tauris, whereas Gerhart Hauptmann was the first to combine the Oresteia with the whole Iphigenia legend, which he completely reshaped. For reasons which we shall try to show, Hauptmann has an Iphigenia at Delphi instead of an Iphigenia in Tauris. To our knowledge no modern interpretation of this story exists—not even a formal or stylistic modernization. Even Hauptmann's work, although it was written in the 1940's, is a traditional verse drama, imitative and old-fashioned in style—which makes it all the more interesting as a document in the history of myth and of modern times. Thus the very existence of this work justifies and even requires its inclusion in the present study, in fact makes it an essential chapter.

Its very existence also explains why the two earlier interpretations of the Iphigenia story, the Greek and the classical German, are reexamined here, although, thanks to Goethe's *Iphigenie,* the comparison is one of the most hackneyed academic themes in literary criticism. They are reexamined not for the sake of completeness (which in any case is not a primary methodological principle of this study) but because of the remarkable and unique literary constellation into which Hauptmann's work throws the earlier Iphigenia plays. Before Hauptmann's House of Atreus tetralogy appeared, Euripides' *Iphigenia in Tauris* was essentially interesting only in the light of Goethe's humanistic play. The latter in turn acquires fresh interest, over and above its own intrinsic immortality, by contrast with Hauptmann rather than Euripides. Although this looks like the traditional contrast that exists between any work of an earlier age and one of our own time, it happens in this case that Hauptmann's modern work also embodies a contrast between the archaic and the humanistic. Goethe's *Iphigenie* thus stands between two manifestations of the archaic : the originally archaic Greek *Iphigenia in Tauris* of Euripides and Hauptmann's modern archaic one. The modern work penetrates more deeply into the ground and background of the archaic spirit than the Greek work itself does; on the other hand, it is more modern than the classic work of German humanism precisely because it is more archaic. Here we have a constellation which makes it profitable to align these three Iphigenia plays, written in 410 B.C., 1786, and 1942, and to assess their particular characteristics.

The decisive line leads from Euripides' *Iphigenia in Tauris* by way of Goethe to Hauptmann. Both Euripides and Hauptmann, however, also wrote an *Iphigenia in Aulis,* and through an odd coincidence in the literary history of this subject they both wrote the play dealing with the first phase of the Iphigenia legend several years after the one dealing with her post-Aulian phase in Tauris or at Dephi. In Hauptmann's case this is obviously explained by the evolution of his conception of the total work. In both cases the Aulis play was the last work of the dramatist's old age. In both cases literary taste—admittedly always subjective—must, or at least tends to, rank the Aulian Iphigenia above the later Taurian or Delphic one. Guided by their dates, let us schematize the treatment of the Iphigenia problem beginning with Euripides' *Iphigenia in Aulis* and closing the circle with Gerhart Hauptmann's play of the same title, thus circumscribing the core problem of the post-Aulian phases so that it can emerge in all its homogeneity and heterogeneity from Euripides via Goethe down to Hauptmann. This will also enable us to present the whole saga chronologically so far as content and theme go, even though we have slightly infringed on the chronological order in which the plays were written.

In the plays dealing with Iphigenia at Aulis the real hero is naturally Iphigenia's father, Agamemnon. It is he who has to act and make decisions, and his position is a terrible one. Euripides skillfully characterized this prince through his situation; he stands out far more forcefully and movingly here than in the Agamemnon plays themselves, the plays dealing with his murder, where he himself is the victim. With great psychological insight Euripides develops the conflict in Agamemnon between ambition as leader of the Achaean army, which entails the obligation to lead it to Troy, and the terrible act of sacrifice with which the words of Calchas have charged him. His indecision comes alive through vivid details. First (in the veiled prehistory) he unhesitatingly sends a letter to his wife summoning her and their daughter and does not shrink from using a deceitful trick, telling them that Achilles has asked for Iphigenia's hand and that the marriage is to be celebrated in his camp. He is then overcome with remorse and sends a second letter to stop them. However, Menelaus, for whom the favor of Artemis is of paramount importance, becomes suspicious and intercepts the letter. In the argument between the two brothers Agamemnon's conflict between paternal love and princely ambition is starkly revealed. His decision is familiar to all of us.

The play is tautly constructed. Halfway through, Agamemnon, who was responsible only for the primary decision, is replaced as the active character (taking *active* in the inward sense of making up one's own mind or of self-determination) by Iphigenia herself. As we said at the beginning, the Iphigenia problem is in itself less productive dramatically than the Orestes theme, because Iphigenia is not in a situation where she must choose and make up her own mind; she is a victim who can only suffer passively. But in making Iphigenia the heroine, Euripides could not have portrayed her merely as a suffering victim having no free will. If she were no more than that, she could not be a tragic heroine; he had to provide her with a heroic dimension.

In the brief course of the action Euripides manages to draw a wonderful picture of the girl's development from the innocent happiness of childhood into a heroine who heroically accepts death. It occurs in three tautly structured stages. First comes her joyous arrival in the camp with her mother, and here the terse dialogue sketches their happy family life and the girl's affectionate love for her father. The second phase is her natural reaction of terror when she learns that she is to be sacrified :

> My body is a suppliant's tight clinging
> To your knees. Do not take away this life
> Of mine before its dying time. Nor make me
> Go down under the earth to see the world
> Of darkness, for it is sweet to look on
> The day's light.[1]

The third phase shows her, more or less reconciled to her father's decision, transcending herself, accepting death for the sake of the honor of her country. But she can achieve this psychological triumph only by bringing home to herself and her parents the significance of her sacrifice, and thus of her own person, for something higher, something beyond the personal :

> O lift up your voices,
> Lift them to Artemis. . . .
> Shout a paean of glory
> To the daughter of Zeus.   (p. 297)

In a beautiful exchange with the chorus of maidens she exalts her
death into a triumphant patriotic action :

> O look at the girl who walks
> To the goddess' altar
> That Troy may be brought low
> And the Phrygian die.
> Behold, she walks
> With her hair in garlands of honor
> And flung upon her body the lustral waters.   (p. 299)

Gerhart Hauptmann criticized this climax in Euripides as an
abrupt, unmotivated reversal from fear of death to heroic decision.[2]
But here his judgment of Euripides is mistaken. Euripides never
created a character which lacked a sound psychological foundation
—in this case, such a foundation is Iphigenia's strongly accentuated
love for her father. It is made very clear that she wants to alleviate
the terrible decision which circumstances have forced upon Agamemnon by accepting her sacrificial death voluntarily and thus
exalting and transfiguring it into a heroic act of patriotism. Schiller,
who translated Euripides' *Iphigenia,* singled out this stroke of
characterization for particular praise : " Can anything be more
momentous and sublime than the sacrifice—and the voluntary sacrifice at that—of a princess in the flower of her youth for the sake of
the happiness of so many assembled nations?"[3] And in fact a dramatist could not have treated this sacrifice in any other way. To have
had Iphigenia dragged, protesting, to the altar would have contra-
vened the aesthetic laws of drama as well as the ethical laws of
character drawing. There had to be a turn of events, a reversal,
stemming from internal and not external causes.

Even according to our own conception of dramaturgy this
play owes its significance and effectiveness to the fact that the *dea
ex machina* does not appear until the sacrifice has been consummated, that Iphigenia's decision is carried out to the bitter end.
It is therefore false to speak of a *dea ex machina* when in the end
the miracle happens and a hind is seen lying on the altar in Iphi-

genia's place, and Artemis informs her mother that the girl has been spirited away and is still alive. This is not a *deus ex machina* solution like those with which other plays of Euripides end, but a true mythical event which continues Iphigenia's story without affecting the deeper ethical and heroic action of the Aulian Iphigenia.

From the dramatic and artistic viewpoint Euripides' *Iphigenia in Tauris* cannot be taken as a direct sequel to his *Iphigenia in Aulis*. As we have said, it was written earlier and lacks the ethical profundity of the later play. Artemis has taken Iphigenia to her shrine in the land of the Taurians and made her her priestess. Artemis was a dark, cruel goddess whose prerogative it was to have every foreigner who came to Tauris killed and sacrificed to her. The priestess had to perform the consecration, if not the slaughter, of the victim, watched over by Thoas, King of the Taurians. All this Iphigenia bitterly recounts in the prologue.

The plot is familiar enough. As a condition of his full expiation Orestes is ordered by Apollo to steal the sacred image of his sister Artemis from the Taurians. With Pylades he reaches the dangerous shore. Orestes and Iphigenia recognize each other and make a plan for escape, which they craftily begin to carry out. It fails and they fall into the hands of Thoas. In the end, however, Athena puts everything right, though not in the way familiar to us from Goethe's *Iphigenia,* by letting Iphigenia go home; she is to become priestess in another shrine of Artemis at Brauron. Only the image of Artemis is to be taken to Delphi and hung in the temple of Apollo; Iphigenia remains in the divine realm of Artemis. The meaning of these facts will not become clear until we come to Hauptmann; in Euripides they remain cryptic and unexplained, and this points to a mythic tradition which had obviously been forgotten by his day and survived only in enigmatic vestiges.

Disregarding for the present the details of mythic history, it is evident that this Taurian Iphigenia is conceived as a much less ethical figure than the Aulian one. It is of course difficult to determine whether and to what extent Euripides intended to present the priestess of Artemis in a somewhat archaic, barbaric light. Ernst Howald, however, does not seem justified in saying that Euripides' Taurian Iphigenia has "stamped herself on human memory as the noblest of the Greek heroines," that "up to the recognition scene she

is noble in every gesture and of the utmost delicacy in her ethics."[4]
To be sure, she complains bitterly about her lot, about being forced
to participate in human sacrifice :

> . . .High Priestess in her temple.
> And still I serve Her on Her festal days.
> Service may seem a holy word. But far
> From holy are these orders I am bound
> To obey, never to question. . . .
> My hands prepare the victims. Other hands,
> There in the inner temple, spill the blood.[5]

But this is the only stirring of Greek *humanitas,* of feminine gentleness, to be seen in her. On the other hand, she shows a very marked
and psychologically quite understandable streak of bitterness and
resentment, directed chiefly against those who are ultimately responsible for her unhappiness and her miserable, drastically changed
existence, Helen and Menelaus. She wishes that a sail may bring
Menelaus and Helen, "my murderess," to Tauris so that her revenge
may overtake them, "another Aulis here for that far-away one,"
that is, retribution for her sacrifice.

Here Euripides' ethos of unvarnished fidelity to reality breaks
through again. Under the influence of a dream which has convinced
her that Orestes is dead, Iphigenia is forced to give up all hope of
deliverance from her exile. She hardens her heart, which, she says,
was formerly gentle and friendly toward strangers :

> For since Orestes is no more alive,
> Now, where my heart was, there is only stone.
> Strangers who come today, no matter who,
> Will find in me a woman beyond tears.
> Unhappiness, O friends, can harden us
> Toward other sorrow harsher than our own.   (p. 135)

This passage occurs just before the arrival of her friends and the
recognition scene. It shows a step in the dehumanization of this
Greek woman who has been thrust into barbarism, although she
still suffers bitterly in the knowledge of her loss—a splendid figure
of a woman, but one who is no longer gentle, no longer fully
humane. We shall now see how the features of archaic existence,
dimly adumbrated by Euripides, are brought out strongly by Hauptmann, the writer of our own time, while in the other great Iphigenia

play, that of Goethe, they are effaced. And there is good reason for this.

Until Hauptmann's *Iphigenia in Delphi* appeared in 1942, Iphigenia implied to the average literary mind Goethe's Iphigenia. Euripides' *Iphigenia in Tauris* was remembered largely as the original of Goethe's adaptation, a source so radically different that it throws into relief Goethe's humanization of the story and the heroine. A first, decisive change is that Goethe's Iphigenia has been able to abolish the custom of human sacrifice, thus making the Taurian world from the outset a humane Iphigenia world, or at any rate a world which can easily be humanized. King Thoas, as a man of eighteenth-century sensibilities, is capable of feeling, of love; an almost idyllic relationship has developed between him and the priestess. She has supported and comforted him in the loss of his son, and he wishes to marry her. Artemis, the dark goddess who appears anything but friendly to Euripides' Iphigenia, becomes Diana, to whom Iphigenia prays as a benevolent rescuer and helper—and when we come to Hauptmann we shall see what an eighteenth-century falsification of mythological history that represents. But to the eighteenth-century mind the gods no longer mean anything. Man and his actions are all that matter, and the deity is nothing more than a copy of man. Iphigenia, embroiled in psychological conflict, begins to doubt the gods :

> O let not opposition start to grow
> Within my bosom. Let it not be torn
> By hatred, like a deadly vulture's claws—
> That same deep hatred which the old-time gods,
> The Titans, hold for you Olympians.
> Save me! And save your image in my mind![6]

And the image of the gods in her mind is saved only because she herself helps truth, goodness, and humanity to triumph. Their image is modeled on the image of justice, goodness, and morality which man bears and cultivates within himself : the ideal of humanity.

The Song of the Fates, which follows the passage cited above, says :

> Let the race of mankind
> Stand in awe of the gods!
> In undying hands

> They hold world dominion,
> With sanction to use it
> As best they see fit.   (lines 1726 ff.)

This song, quoted by Iphigenia, has a profound meaning. Through the splendid image of enthroned gods casting Tantalus down from his golden seat, it illuminates the secular turning point at which man has found his way out of his archaic subjection, out of his belief in powers which arbitrarily rule him, and has attained himself, and awareness of his own self, of his manhood and his morality —awareness of his own divinity, that is to say, his humanity. It is important to note that Iphigenia recites the Song of the Fates as a quotation, as something not her own, something she has brought up out of her memory. "When we were babes our nurse would sing it to me," she says, and even when the nurse sang it it was an old song, telling of things long past.

The song occurs at the end of the fourth act, just when the old era, the archaic world of human sacrifice, threatens to revive and annihilate the new Iphigenia world. It revives in Thoas, who, feeling that he has been betrayed, angrily proposes to offer up Orestes and Pylades in a sacrifice which, he says, has already been too long withheld from the goddess. But even in Thoas the old spirit does not reemerge in its original archaic form but as a regression from an already civilized stage of life. Its eruption is in fact explained by his having become civilized and thus susceptible to the inner hurt he experiences when Iphigenia rejects his suit, gently as she does it.

Structurally the Song of the Fates occurs exactly at the point when, in the fifth act, the humanistic light is about to break through definitively and the Iphigenia world is established once and for all, even overcoming the temptation, to which the terrible force of circumstances has exposed Iphigenia herself, to escape secretly with her supporters, to lie to and deceive the husband who has trusted her and become "her second father." The triumph of humanity humanized and of the principles and ideas which inspire it—truth, mutual trust, repudiation of lies and of all selfish, utilitarian conduct, rejection of the idea that the end justifies the means (the determining principle in Euripides' Iphigenia)—all this is now achieved in full measure and epitomized in the classic lines of the classic age of German humanism :

>Accursed lies! Lies do not liberate
>The heart like other truly spoken words.
>They bring no comfort; rather they torment
>The man who fashions them in secret.
>And like an arrow which a god deflects
>To miss its target, they return
>To kill the bowman.   (lines 1405 ff.)

Iphigenia prevails upon Thoas through the truth. She places her own fate and that of her friends in his hand and does not rest until he lets her go in friendship with the simple word "Farewell." This scene, famous in the history of German humanism and humanistic literature, needs no further commentary.

As we have already said, Gerhart Hauptmann's House of Atreus cycle, the *Atridentetralogie,* created a new frame of comparison in which the humanistic idea presented in Gothe's Iphigenia acquires a different kind of forcefulness from that which previous comparisons with Euripides' play had given it. This time the significant point is what it loses, not what it gains, in the comparison.

The House of Atreus tetralogy, the final work of Hauptmann's old age, completed in 1945, introduced into literature a totally new phase of the Iphigenia legend. Although, as the title indicates, the work deals with the whole saga of the Atridae, it centers on Iphigenia and the Iphigenia problem, as the order in which the individual plays were written shows. The first, the origin of the whole conception, was *Iphigenie in Delphi* (1942), which was to become the last play in the tetralogy. The three plays dealing with what had gone before, *Iphigenie in Aulis, Agamemnons Tod (Agamemnon's Death*), and *Elektra,* were written later, between 1943 and 1945. As the titles indicate, the play that introduces new subject matter is the last one, the one that was written first. It provides the basis on which the thematic problem of the whole work rests, and this problem departs radically from those of the earlier Iphigenia plays.

Hauptmann did not invent his material; it had already been used by other dramatists who got it from the same source as he used, or which at any rate called his attention to the legend :[7] a remark of Goethe's in the *Italian Journey.*[8] Goethe himself had discovered the legend in the *Fabulae* of Hyginus, the Roman mythologist.[9] Hyginus relates how Iphigenia, with Orestes and Pylades, brings the image of Artemis to Delphi, as she has been ordered to do. Electra has also come to Delphi to lay the axe with which Clytemnestra was killed on Apollo's altar in atonement. After some dangerous episodes in which Electra's impetuous passions again play a role (falsely informed of Orestes' death in Tauris, she jumps to the conclusion that Iphigenia, the priestess, has murdered him, and raises the axe to kill her), the sisters recognize one another and all four return to Argos. However, this factual material is not the decisive new element in Hauptmann's work, which follows Hyginus except for the ending, the joyful return. What is new is the conception of the Iphigenia figure itself, and even this cannot be called Hauptmann's invention, since it derives from contemporary research into the Iphigenia myth.[10]

Iphigenia's story, as the familiar tragedies tell it, is in itself most remarkable. In a manner unique in Greek mythology, a goddess intervenes in her life, snatches her from the sacrificial altar, and installs her as a priestess. But what we have here are the vestiges of an Iphigenia myth in which, far from being the daughter of Agamemnon, she was a chthonian goddess like Hecate, a goddess of birth but also a baneful goddess of death identified with Hecate herself or, according to another tradition, changed by Artemis into Hecate and thus made immortal.

Hecate, herself, however, was not just Artemis under another name; she was originally a separate deity, a dark, bloody goddess of night and death, whose realm was the realm of primeval fear, of the archaic, chthonian spirit. In early times she was identified with Artemis and merged in her cult, later to be completely supplanted by the Olympian goddess, daughter of Zeus and sister of Apollo. Instead of being goddess of night, she was now only the brighter goddess of the moon and also of the hunt, and the patroness of women in childbirth. No doubt Iphigenia became associated with Hecate through her connection with the saga of the Atridae, as Agamemnon's daughter who was sacrificed, and through the events at Aulis and the role which Artemis played there. The Hecatean side of Artemis, that is, her archaic phase, as well as Iphigenia's mythic connection with Hecate and her own Hecatean divine nature, emerges in the story of her sacrifice and in the bloody rites she celebrates (albeit under duress) as a priestess, which survived as vestiges of her original legend.

When we realize that Iphigenia's story was originally that of a goddess, not a mortal, her literary history becomes extremely interesting. In Euripides we can find even more obvious traces of her connection with the Hecatean Artemis : not only her celebration of human sacrifices but, more indicative still, the fact that in the end she is merely transferred to another shrine of Artemis and does not return to her real, human home in the land of the Atridae. However, these vestiges are not cogently related and must therefore be unconscious. In Goethe they have been largely eliminated, dispersed, as it were, in the climate of humanism. Drawing upon the greater knowledge of the myth which post-Goethe research had provided, Gerhart Hauptmann for the first time exposed the archaic background of the Iphigenia figure, depicting it literally in the priestess who reaches Delphi with Orestes and Pylades, and at the same time making it a symbol of human existence.

The Iphigenia who arrives in Delphi is still, to be sure, the sister of Orestes and Electra, the former Greek princess; there is a recognition scene. But instead of a joyful, intimate, human reunion, there is on Iphigenia's part only coldness and a refusal to return home with her brother and sister. The priestess has the features of a goddess. "She is taller than the others," say the stage directions, "and wears a fixed, archaic smile." But even before she appears, the three old men who speak for the people of Delphi are muttering among themselves :

> . . . goddess of death,
> the torch-bearer, the huntress, in a word
> inexorable Hecate herself
> stands before Delphi's gates, beseeching them
> to let her in.[11]

When she arrives in Delphi and recognizes her brother and sister, when memories of her mortal past arise, she feels for a moment that she may still be a mortal capable of human feeling :

> You, my goddess! O, my mother! You! . . .
> The stubborn ore from which you cast my soul
> Begins to melt. The secret core within
> Becomes less rigid. What seemed dead like me
> Now stirs and moves as though it were alive. (p. 249)

But the impulse is only momentary. Hauptmann does not allow

himself any further departures from the Hecatean nature of the priestess—a conception new to world literature which he created in this work. This Iphigenia actually did perform the rites of human sacrifice in Tauris; no impulse of tenderness ever deterred her, as it deterred Euripides' Iphigenia.

The change Hauptmann makes in the Taurian events is also significant. No recognition scene with Orestes occurs there; that is to say, in Tauris Iphigenia never feels even the merest trace of awareness of her mortal past. All she is aware of is her terrible divinity and non-human nature. Even when Agamemnon's name falls upon her ear, when Orestes, not yet having recognized her, mentions the sacrifice at Aulis, she does not—will not—recognize herself as the woman she used to be. She rejects even the faintest glimmer of potential memory :

> For all that throngs and clings about me here
> Falls dead, prostrated by my priestly robes.
> They say a virgin once was sacrificed
> Upon the altar of the goddess. True,
> The same thing happened long ago to me.
> I have no wish to know the truth of it.
> This is enough: dying made me a part
> Of the divine; I do not choose
> Ever to live a mortal life again.   (p. 245)

This is a divinity foreign and hostile to the human and to humankind—anti-humane in the true sense. The goddess to whom she prays is not the gentle Diana of Goethe's Iphigenia; she does not pray, as Goethe's Iphigenia does, to be released from her priest-hood and allowed to go home. She asks to be taken back :

> Into the wilds of some barbaric land,
> Or, if that may not be, then where thou willst
> Remote from people, revelry and joy—
> All loathsome to me as a baby's pap.
> Away! Into some mountain cave or desert waste,
> Where none can penetrate my solitude.   (p. 250)

She is not praying to Artemis but still to Hecate. And within the context of this work the word "still" used in this way (or the words "not yet" applied to Artemis) suggests the secular turning

point which is the real theme of this Iphigenia play : the overthrow
of the archaic cult of Hecate by the Delphic cult of Apollo. It is no
accident that the play is set in Delphi, center of the cult of Apollo.
Among its most beautiful scenes is the entrance of the Delphic
priests, who know that the turning point is at hand when Artemis
will cast off for good her archaic Hecatean form and reign as a pure
Olympian, sister of Apollo. The theft of the image of Artemis from
Tauris, the realm of Hecate, and its removal to Delphi at Apollo's
command, which occurs in a germinal form in all the Taurian
Iphigenia plays, acquires its significance as a historical religious
event for the first time in Hauptmann's *Iphigenia in Delphi*. The
priests know that the hour is at hand for the coming of a more
humane spirit which will supersede the Hecatean spirit in man's
consciousness. They prepare to celebrate the reconciliation between
Artemis and Apollo, the mythological and symbolical manifestation
of this radical change :

> These rites, this feast of feasts we now prepare
> Betoken reconciliation.
> Heaven proclaims the news throughout the world
> That Artemis and Phoebus, long at odds,
> Are reunited in fraternal love.   (p. 238)

But what is Iphigenia's position? Her return to Delphi with
the image of Artemis might—in fact should—mean that she too is
to be allowed to discard her Hecatean form and return to a human,
mortal one. This is also the scholarly explanation of her remarkable
dual myth as a Hecatean goddess and later as Agamemnon's
daughter. To quote Pauly-Wissowa : "The religious and cultural
evolution of Iphigenia as a deity was probably closely connected
with the advance of the cult of Apollo and the religious movement
emanating from Delphi, which may well have opposed primitive
archaic rites, especially human sacrifice."[12] Although the play's very
existence and the title *Iphigenia in Delphi* might indicate a meta-
morphosis of this kind, its content shows that the title actually
denotes the opposite : that Iphigenia's arrival in Delphi comes too
late and the priestess of Hecate neither can nor will become the
priestess of Artemis. She prayed to Hecate to allow her to return to
her realm of the dead and she knows that a new day is dawning in
which she has no part :

I have been told that Hecate, now linked
more closely with Apollo, means to found
a cult in Hellas. And I fear
that Hecate thus changed will need a change
of priestess.   (p. 244)

The play, and with it the tetralogy, ends with Iphigenia throwing herself from a cliff, that is, symbolically returning to Hecate's
realm of the dead from which she came.

These are just facts, which provide no more than a starting
point for investigating the meaning of this Iphigenia work. It may
be asked—in fact the question almost poses itself—why Iphigenia
too does not adapt herself to the new era, why she does not follow
her goddess in her transformation into a pure Artemis, why, if she
prefers not to go home with her brother and sister, she does not
dedicate herself to the service of the Delphic Apollo instead of
Hecate. We have now reached the point from which we can look
into the symbolic meaning which Hauptmann injected into the
archaic Iphigenia myth and its mythologically obscure and enigmatic duality. Although his treatment of the myth is the first in
literature to capture its true archaic character and although he
broadened it to reveal an important new facet of the history of
ideas, he nevertheless interpreted its archaic aspect in a way which
can only be called extremely modern.

A humanistic age could take the triumph of the Delphic spirit
over the archaic one for a final victory and cherish the belief that
man consistently progresses from the lower to the higher. Scientific
evidence as well as the brutal events of our own time have taught
us that "the archaic," sublimated or repressed as it may be, has not
been completely overcome and may erupt again at any time and
become terribly contemporary. Although mythology tells us that
Iphigenia-Hecate yielded to the new Delphic spirit, the plot of
Hauptmann's tetralogy shows that Hecate's realm does not pass
away but remains. This Iphigenia dies "into the divine" a second
time; she returns to Hecate's realm of the dead to preserve her own
Hecatean, chthonian godhead, a "subhuman" godhead alien and
antithetical to the classical Apollonian divinity. Her death has the
profound symbolic meaning that the domain of life personified in
her Hecatean godhead is always with us.[13] Hauptmann did not
merely reinstate something which the evolution of the legend itself

and its treatment in literature had reduced to a mere vestige of its
original form : Iphigenia's sacrifice at Aulis and her priesthood
among the Taurians; he also revealed its elemental, tragic, significance as an essential symbol.

It may seem in some way inappropriate to see in the noble,
sublime form of the priestess, once a lovely Greek princess, a personification of bloody Hecate of whom Orestes says :

> A woman preternaturally cruel,
> Is priestess to the bloody goddess.
> This monster speaks in the Ionic tongue. . . .
> Within her slaughterhouse she reigns supreme,
> More cruel, merciless and bloodthirsty
> Than Hecate herself.   (pp. 225 ff.)

Yet it is precisely this terrible duality of Iphigenia, Greek princess
and Hecatean goddess, the duality of the humane and the infernal,
the chthonian, that symbolizes human existence. Agamemnon's
lovely daughter, forced to become and remain for ever Hecate, is a
tragic figure, tragic in the same sense as human existence, which she
symbolizes.

> He who has once been chosen by a god
> For sacrifice may think he has escaped,
> But all in vain. The Fates will seek him out,
> Wherever he may hide, and bring him back
> To that same altar which but now he fled.   (p. 270)

The priests, who understand and who are actively promulgat-
ing a new spirit, are only too aware of the presence, the power, and
the danger of the old one. All they can do is admonish the younger
priests, the disciples, to whom they dare not reveal the tragic secret,
to fortify their souls unceasingly "in piety and submission to the
will of God."

We have so far only been dealing with the second half of
Iphigenia in Delphi, the part which shapes and interprets the
Iphigenia myth in a completely untraditional way and which was
therefore the logical starting point for our analysis. By contrast, the
first half of the final play of the tetralogy conforms entirely to the
tradition of the *Oresteia,* which Hauptmann followed. The fact that
Orestes and Electra come to Delphi and are freed of their guilt by

the Delphic god and the kindly spirit for which he stands in no way alters their traditional character. Within the work's structure and meaning the first half of *Iphigenia in Delphi* is linked with the two central plays, *Agamemnon's Death* and *Electra,* that is to say, with the chain of events which they relate : the murder of the husband, the matricide, and the expiation (the counterpart of Aeschylus' *Oresteia*). The structure and meaning of the whole work is significantly illuminated when we recognize that the second half of the last play, the Iphigenia story, is connected with the *Oresteia* only through Iphigenia's being brought to Delphi by Orestes and Pylades. Traditionally, and in all earlier versions, the plot was meant to culminate in the happy reunion of brother and sister. Here, on the contrary, Orestes is merely the instrument through which a mythical, symbolical event happens to and through Iphigenia. Orestes' and Electra's destinies are fulfilled quite independently of this.

Between the first and second halves of the final play—and consequently between the second half and all the preceding plays of the tetralogy—there exists a connection which is by no means a mere cause-and-effect linking of events but an occult relationship arising entirely out of the symbolic meaning of the Iphigenia figure itself. There is no doubt that Hauptmann first became aware of this in dealing with the Delphic phase, when the archaic mythical figure arrives at the birthplace of the new humanism. Unquestionably what inspired his conception of the plays dealing with the prehistory, especially *Iphigenia in Aulis,* was the idea of depicting on a more elaborate scale of action and imagery the secular turning point which in these few scenes builds up and culminates, as it were, in one single mythic act.[14] *Iphigenia in Aulis,* whose ambience is also that of *Agamemnon's Death* and *Electra,* is without doubt one of the most powerful plays of our time. It may, in fact, be called a contemporary document of a most cryptic nature, however "unmodern" its style, diction, form, and even its psychology may be. A short survey of these three plays will not only be germane to Hauptmann's understanding of the Iphigenia problem, but will also round out the cycle of Iphigenia plays which began with Euripides' *Iphigenia in Aulis.* Hauptmann's *Iphigenia in Aulis,* however, reveals its full meaning only in the light of his *Iphigenia in Delphi.*

The time of *Iphigenia in Aulis* is still the time of Hecate, suggestively evoked right at the outset :

> A haunted atmosphere of waking sleep
> And sleeping wakefulness. This evil dream—
> When will it end and where? The horrid corpselike
> Light of the moon goddess, feeding on graves—
> This is its milk. Who can help but feel
> Hades pervading all our mortal world?   (p. 7)

The ship which has appeared in the bay of Aulis, "black, with grotesque red masks on its black sails," proclaims a resurgence of the Hecatean spirit in an age which is striving slowly and painfully to escape from it:

> It comes from Tauris from the goddess
> Who feasts on human blood. Who does not shake
> In terror at the name of Hecate?   (p. 11)

Primeval fear seems to spread throughout the play, and in the darkness of this historic hour, when a new age is just beginning to dawn on the horizon, the personages assume mighty but still uncertain contours. Agamemnon and Clytemnestra, for example, are still drawn to an archaic, titanic scale. In these monumental figures primeval human drives, primal human nature itself, seem to take shape: lust for power, ambition, and masculine desire for sovereignty in Agamemnon, prince of the nations; in Clytemnestra, motherhood, stronger than conjugal love is the husband-murderer whom the dramatist of this chthonian world has, as it were, sanctified in a creatural sense. More decisively than ever before, Clytemnestra's act of murder is motivated entirely by the mortal insult to her maternal instinct. This Clytemnestra is convincing, not hypocritical, in maintaining that the sacrifice of her daughter destroyed once and for all her heartfelt loyalty to her husband.

But even though this primitive instinctiveness is, as it were, still admitted to the chthonian ground of being, people are nonetheless already rising above it. For the secular turning point is at hand when the Hecatean world will be driven back and men liberated from their instincts and fears. The battle of the eras is already under way, or so it seems, when the truly dramatic—and in Sartre's sense existential—conflict begins: Agamemnon's struggle with his conscience and the "choice" which drives him into utterly destructive conflict not only with Clytemnestra but also with himself.

But Hauptmann does not rely on these central characters alone

to bring the "naïve" events of ancient Greek tradition into the
awareness of this secular turning point. He also uses two others :
the nurse Peitho and Calchas, the seer. Peitho is a figure who stands
on the borderline between the two eras. It is no accident that she,
whose mother still served Hecate, is the attendant of the radiant
Greek girl Iphigenia. Endowed with the dark gift of prophecy and
versed in chthonian magic, still close to the primeval, embodying
existential anxiety, Peitho has come to accept the view of those she
serves. At Clytemnestra's side she opposes Agamemnon, the origina-
tor of all the tragedy, who stands for regression to barbarism.

In Calchas the topicality of Hauptmann's work becomes most
evident and most direct—though only intermittently because the
character of Calchas lacks consistency. He is not characterized
purely in the antique spirit of the legend, for here Hauptmann is
quite obviously alluding to the barbaric regression he had had to
live through in his own country and to the man responsible for it.
The famous seer is shown as a somewhat suspect figure, a power-
hungry man thrown up by the ferment within the populace. Both
Menelaus and Clytemnestra accuse him of craftily reviving the
archaic instincts of the people and manipulating them to exert
pressure on lords and princes. A man who

> Seeks to revive a cruel, long dead rite
> Of brutish peoples: human sacrifice,
> Rampant in Tauris still, still solemnized
> In that dread temple of wild cannibals.
> Woe betide Hellas if he once succeed!   (p. 46)

In the Aulian phase of her history Iphigenia herself, the most
beautiful princess of Greece, can of course have nothing in common
with the priestess of Hecate, the archaic deity of Delphi. She is the
purest image of Apollonian human beauty, the most radiant figure
in her whole environment, standing out against the still dark background of the Hecatean world. But the very presence of this background already stamps Hauptmann's Aulian Iphigenia with her
special character and suggests what she stands for—something that
was conceived in the light of the Delphic Iphigenia and that reveals
itself fully only in her. Behind Agamemnon's daughter and Achilles'
bride (and here the betrothal is presented as a genuine love match)
the divine, mythic design, whose exact nature is not yet clear,

already begins to unfold. Iphigenia's final acceptance of her sacrifice stems not merely from heroic, patriotic feelings but from an inkling of her divine descent and her divine future, the real truth of her life.

> I never knew till now what truth might be.
> Descending from on high, omnipotent,
> It fills me. O, pray Heaven not to let
> This sacred vessel shatter into shards.
> To feel such truth within me is to die
> Or be reborn out of the common herd,
> And jubilantly enter the divine.   (p. 82)

But the design becomes clearer; the sinister nature of this goddess begins to emerge in the dream in which she appears to Achilles :

> . . .calling herself
> Daughter of Agamemnon, then again
> Persephone, and even, strangest of all,
> Giving herself the name of Hecate.   (p. 88)

"Humanity and godhead now begin to fuse. / The sacred climes of Hades and Olympus mingle," proclaims Agamemnon during the solemn preparations for the sacrifice.

The central plays of the tetralogy, *Agamemnon's Death* and *Electra,* need to be considered only briefly and only insofar as they bear on the Iphigenia problem (although of course Iphigenia does not appear in them). They have another function in the structure of the tetralogy besides that of developing the plot. The sacrifice of Iphigenia meant that in the battle of the eras the "olden days," the world of Hecate, had triumphed once again. In the Oresteia plays the eruption of barbarism is consolidated, so to speak. The rustic mountain temple of Demeter, the room used for ritual baths, with its three primitive cult images representing the chthonian goddesses of the earth, the underworld, and Hades : Demeter, Pluto, and Core—this is the scene of the familiar episode. The participants, Clytemnestra, Aegisthus, Cassandra, and Electra, seem to have sunk back to the bottommost depths of instinctual life, into adultery, revenge, hatred, and lust for killing. This "darkness of a starless night," which the stage directions accentuate symbolically, will soon be unbroken by even the faintest glimmer of humanity or gentleness.

In order to bring this out, another new character is introduced :

Thestor, father of Calchas, who nevertheless holds aloof from his "terrible son" and represents a final attempt of some sort to hold on to humanity. But his still hopeful words to Orestes, Electra, and Pylades pointing toward a brighter future are engulfed in the ghastly cycle of murder, revenge, and murder which now begins and, as we have said, continues well into the redemption play, *Iphigenia in Delphi.*

Thus from this viewpoint too we see the significance of Hauptmann's idea of following the Oresteia story with an Iphigenia in Delphi instead of a traditional Iphigenia in Tauris. Delphi is the holy place which can supersede and annul Tauris. In Goethe's *Iphigenia in Tauris,* only Orestes could be redeemed, and only by Iphigenia herself. In Hauptmann, Iphigenia's function is performed by Delphi, and Iphigenia herself becomes a mythical symbol of the existential problems of human history. For Orestes and Electra Delphi is the holy place of expiation and redemption, and this in itself indicates that the scope of the traditional Taurian story has been broadened to stand for human history in general. Hauptmann shows this in dramatic, visual form by introducing the Delphic shrine, where the archaic, chthonian world gives way to the humane one, just as it did long ago in the *Eumenides* of Aeschylus. The linking of the *Oresteia* with the "new" archaic Iphigenia myth, unprecedented in literature, reveals its meaning: behind the redemption of Orestes, and consequently of the House of Atreus, there still persists the dark horizon symbolized by the priestess Hecate.

We have attempted to show the significance of the fact that Iphigenia does not go home with her brother and sister as tradition relates, but becomes the vehicle for an incident of mythic death. By freeing her from her brother's and sister's world and history, by removing her, in fact, altogether from the human world into which the evolution of her legend had, so to speak, dragged her, and by restoring her to the stature of a mythical figure, the dramatist enlarges the human historical scope of his work by that archaic dimension of which our time has been the first to regain awareness. That Iphigenia does not return to the human world but, by sacrificing herself, retains her own somber divinity, may be taken as a symbolic way of saying that that which is inimical to man, that which is anti-humane, the death and the fear inherent in the Hecatean world, has not been completely dissolved in the humane but still persists, no matter how forgotten or repressed, in the depths and hidden recesses of the historical human world, ready at all times to break out anew. Such was the cryptic, pessimistic message which the aged Gerhart Hauptmann handed down in his final work in the symbol of Iphigenia, who is at one and the same time an Apollonian, humane figure and a Hecatean deity.

5

HELEN

Before leaving the tremendous saga of the Atridae, let us speak a little of Helen the beautiful, that fascinating carrier of doom who is associated with this legend if only as the original cause of the tragedy of the House of Atreus, insofar as that tragedy was precipitated by the Trojan War. Many common features link her history with that of her niece Iphigenia. Like Iphigenia, Helen towers above the mortal setting of the Atridae saga into a mythic sphere; she too is surrounded by mystery. But within the likeness there are differences, not only in the myths themselves but in the existence of these figures and the roles they play in Greek mythology.

The age of the Greek tragedians was no longer aware of Iphigenia's dark death myth; it survived in their works only vestigially. Helen's legend, on the other hand, belongs to the bright Olympian mythology from which they regularly drew their themes. There she is first of all a demigoddess, like so many heroes and heroines of this mythology : daughters or sons of mortal women by Zeus, the father of the gods, who was so susceptible to the feminine charms of mortals. Helen, as we know, was the daughter of Leda, to whom Zeus came in the form of a swan, and the sister of Clytemnestra (through her earthly stepfather Tyndareus, Leda's husband).

The tragedians, however—and Euripides is the only one we need to consider in connection with the Helen theme—were not concerned with these matters. To them this was the way things were; they accepted such circumstances as a matter of fact, involving no particular problems and no deeper implications. Whether Helen was a demigoddess or a mortal was irrelevant for judging her as an individual, for assessing her behavior toward Menelaus and Paris and the fact that she caused the war. In the prologue to Euripides' *The Trojan Women* Poseidon speaks of her as a daughter of Tyndareus, that is, purely in her earthly capacity, and in this play, which depicts the grim, cruel fate of the royal women of Troy, now slaves of the Greek princes, Helen is, understandably, nothing but an object of hatred and recrimination, in Hecuba's words :

> the fatal bride
> of Menelaus, Castor her brother's shame
> the stain on the Eurotas.
> Now she has killed
> the sire of the fifty sons,
> Priam; me, unhappy Hecuba
> she drove on this reef of ruin.[1]

Her excuse that Aphrodite, determined to make Paris award her the apple, promised him Helen as a reward is rejected as a lie. Even Menelaus is by no means overjoyed at the prospect of getting her back and in fact proposes to have her stoned. That she is nevertheless saved from death is explained by certain other myths which have grown up around this controversial figure and which a modern eye may well identify as an image of her mysterious essence, the secret of beauty itself. The tragedians could not conceive of Helen as a mythic manifestation of an idea, as an *eidos*. They were dealing with something handed down to them as fact, even though it may have been the fact of myth.

A modern view may be seen in that subtle, profound play of Giraudoux, *La guerre de Troie n'aura pas Lieu* (*Tiger at the Gates*), in which, through the example of the Trojan War, he brings home to us the ultimately irrational causes of wars. Here Helen is the central character, since the fruitless debate whether the "gate of war" can be kept closed or not flares up over the possibility of giving her back, as the concrete reason for the threat of war, to the Greeks besieging the gates of Troy. But let us ignore the message of Giraudoux's play for the moment and look simply at the figure of Helen. It is hardly necessary to point out that here, as in all the modern French dramatists' Greek plays, the high tragedy has been stripped of its loftiness and pathos and reduced to everyday human dimensions. In a sense the play is a counterpart of Euripides' *Trojan Women*. The fact that the thematic scene—and it really is no more than that—which in Euripides' play takes place after the war, occurs in Giraudoux before its outbreak is what makes it possible to eliminate the pathos, because the catastrophe has not yet broken forth. But in both cases the important thing is not action but discussion, bitter and sorrowful in Euripides, reasonable and sometimes ironical in Giraudoux. Hecuba, in Euripides crushed by a terrible fate, is in Giraudoux a resolute ruler and mother. In both cases she is Helen's bitterest enemy.

Even here Helen herself is not idealized or mythicized. Even her beauty is not particularly effective any more, except upon the elderly gentlemen, especially Priam. "Give her back to the Greeks quickly if you want her to symbolize beauty much longer," says matter-of-fact Hecuba. "She's a blonde, after all."[2] Despite the ironical treatment and sober relativization of Helen's beauty and her role, Giraudoux does let us glimpse the aura of mystery which surrounds this ultimate archetype of beauty and which has embodied itself in the myth of her divine origin. She is not so clearly profiled as the other level-headed people in this play. In the final analysis she wants no part in anything or anybody. She submits to love, not caring who her partner may be.

We recognize in this erotic flightiness a divine element which Giraudoux had already made the theme of his *Electra*: the profound and absolute indifference of the gods, whom man quite mistakenly thinks he can relate to himself. There is something of this in Giraudoux's Helen too. "The word *pity*! That's not my line," she says to Andromache. "I'm not much good at pity" (p. 420). And yet she is not so simple and transparent after all. She immediately adds that she is very much at home with unhappy people—and, oddly enough, exactly at this point we are offered a glimpse of her mythic nature. "I used to take birds out of their nests and raise them. I'm descended from a bird—I suppose that's why I'm so mad about them. I know all about all the mishaps to the human body that have anything to do with birds: the father's body cast up by the morning tide, quite stiff, with a head which gets bigger and bigger because the seagulls are flocking to peck the eyes out. . . .My little friend with the goldfinch was a hunchback. And my little

friend with the bullfinch was consumptive" (p. 420). Here the
Olympian descent of Zeus as a swan is transformed into an existential form of being which might be called nature mysticism and
which is equally indifferent to all psychological and ethical factors
on which specifically human life is based.

We have linked Giraudoux directly to Euripides in order to
expose one of the lines running through the various interpretations
of Helen, a line which may be epitomized in the question : What
about beauty? But the answer given in the greatest Helen play in
world literature, the third act of Goethe's *Faust*, Part II, cannot be
drawn into our argument. For we could only indicate what Goethe's
Helen represents in the context of his Faust tragedy : the ideal of
classical beauty, of Greek antiquity itself, which this "classical-
romantic phantasmagoria" fuses, for one single moment in Faust's
striving existence, with the Nordic-romantic ideal for which Faust
stands in this act of the play. Yet Goethe's Helen too knows what
beauty means when not exalted to an idea but humanly embodied
in the most beautiful of women, "the much admired and much
upbraided Helen." She puts it very plainly :

> Singly the world I troubled, doubly more so,
> Now triply, fourfold I add woe to woe.[3]

There also exists, however, a Helen myth which undertakes to
rehabilitate this much upbraided woman and to reveal the irresponsible adulteress as a loyal, honorable wife. This legend of the
Egyptian Helen was recounted by Stesichorus in the sixth century
and dramatized by Euripides in his *Helen*. The prologue, spoken in
Euripides' play by Helen herself, outlines the state of affairs, and
here again she tries to make herself appear the innocent victim of
divine jealousy. When Paris came to Sparta to claim Helen as his
wife (promised to him by Aphrodite in return for awarding her the
apple), Hera, offended at not having won the prize herself, inter-
vened and caused him to take a phantom back to Troy instead of
the real Helen. On this account, Helen bitterly laments, war broke
out. She herself was taken by Hermes to King Proteus on the island
of Pharos in Egypt, where she has remained true to her husband
Menelaus, despite all the assaults made upon her virtue, after the
old king's death, by his son Theoclymenus, whose advances she has
steadfastly resisted. She has just learned from the good prophetess

Theonoe, sister of Theoclymenus, that Menelaus, whose death she had reluctantly come to accept, is alive. At this point (that is, after the end of the war) Menelaus has just been shipwrecked on the coast of Pharos—in company of course with the phantom Helen whom he has brought back from Troy, believing her to be his wife.

It is not difficult to imagine the confusion that ensues, although the two Helens do not, in fact, meet. Menelaus has hidden his phantom in a mountain cave and appears alone at the palace gate, somewhat astonished to be told by the portress that "Cronus' daughter Helen dwells within," and thinking for a moment that his wife has been abducted from the mountain cave. The confusion is not diminished when Menelaus and Helen actually meet and recognize each other, but is soon dispelled by the news that the phantom has been "invisibly wafted up to Heaven." Menelaus can now recognize the true Helen as the real one, the one who has always been his, always faithful to him.

Euripides' *Helen* has been equated with his *Iphigenia in Tauris,* and indeed there are thematic and structural parallels. In both plays somebody is spirited away (though in *Helen* in a less drastic manner); those who have been separated find and recognize one another; and finally—the true dramatic crux—there is an escape from a threatening situation and a happy return home. Theoclymenus here plays the role of Thoas, the one who has to be out-witted. The ruse, planned and executed much as the one in *Iphigenia* is, succeeds immediately, and there is nothing left for the *deus ex machina* (in the form of Helen's demigod brothers) to do but protect the good Theonoe, who had stood by them, from the anger and the sword of Theoclymenus.

Even this short resume will show that ethically and spiritually this Egyptian *Helen* surpasses *Iphigenia in Tauris.* The originality of the conception itself should not be overlooked : the idea that somebody who has been unjustly defamed should be rehabilitated. This theme is quite plainly expressed in the play. Nothing hurts Helen more than having her name dishonored by the shame of having caused the war :

> Because of me, beside the waters of Scamander, lives
> were lost in numbers; and the ever patient I
> am cursed by all and thought to have betrayed my lord
> and for the Hellenes lit the flame of a great war.   (p. 192)

Conjugal love and loyalty are plainly the ethos of this play, whose key scenes are the ones in which Helen and Menelaus declare their love for one another. The success of their ruse and their escape through their own efforts, without the help of a *deus ex machina,* can be taken to mean that when man is strong and self-reliant he does not need the help of the gods.

Two interpretations exist of this legend, which Euripides made famous; both are in the German language : Hofmannsthal's poetic treatment in his opera libretto *Die ägyptische Helena (The Egyptian Helen)* and a few pages in a philosophical work, the section entitled "Utopischer Bildrest in der Verwirklichung. Ägyptische und Trojanische Helena" ("Utopian Image Residue. Egyptian and Trojan Helen") in Ernst Bloch's *Das Prinzip Hoffnung,* written about 1940. The latter, although not strictly relevant to our present theme, which is confined to Greek figures in dramatic literature, deserves discussion here because it offers an extremely interesting contrast to Hofmannsthal's version. Moreover, the nature of Bloch's interpretation is such that it might well provide the conceptual basis for a literary work on this subject.

Bloch thinks that "the essentially fragmentary subject matter [of Euripides' play] deserves in the succession treatment by a Shakespeare but has not found even a Hebbel."[4] In his opinion Hofmannsthal's work did not fill the gap; without Strauss's music, he says disparagingly, it is of little significance. We may pass over the value judgment. The interesting point for our context is that Bloch interprets the story of the dual Helen as a mythic, archetypal image of the "Utopian dream longing" which is given with human existence. Even though the legend says that the Egyptian Helen is the real one and the Trojan Helen only a phantom, the deep truth is that the brutal reality of the war did come about for the sake of the phantom. "Only the Trojan Helen, not the Egyptian one, followed the flag, went through the yearnings of the ten Utopian years, the cuckold's love-hatred, the many nights spent far from home, the rough military camps, and the foretaste of victory" (p. 212). In comparison with this true reality of the eidolon, "the Egyptian reality as such is of a lower order," says Bloch (p. 213). He interprets the "wisp of fiery air"[5] in which Helen vanishes as the surviving vestige of the higher, Utopian reality which is never attained by actual reality but which nevertheless represents "the element hope," which, ideal as it may be, "is never completely beyond the objective potentialities of reality. Thus the essence of the Trojan Helen is pretraced in the Egyptian one" (p. 213).

Bloch might have cited Western literary tradition in support of his thesis that the phantom Helen whom the Helen-in-Egypt myth represents as non-real is actually the real one. In this tradition the Trojan Helen alone has survived, as a mythological reality, not as a phantom or a shadow, and has become a creative prototypal figure—Helen the beautiful, to whom erotic flightiness emblematically belongs, as it does to Paris.

There is nothing to contradict this view in the fourth book of the *Odyssey,* where Helen, virtuous wife and princess, now reunited in mutual fidelity with Menelaus, greets Telemachus when he comes to the Spartan court on his voyage in search of his father. Hofmannsthal, as well as Bloch, refers to this passage, which, together with Euripides' *Helen,* became the germ of his lyrical libretto. In an essay on the Egyptian Helen written in 1928, a commentary on his own work, he says that this passage in Homer prompted his imagination to ask what might have happened between that night in Troy which Homer describes, when "without a word Menelaus carried this woman, who even in this situation was still the most beautiful woman in the world, out of the city, down to the sea and aboard his ship"[6] and the peaceful scene between the two of them in the fourth book of the *Odyssey.* "What a situation for a husband!" he exclaims, for, after all, Helen was the cause of the war, besides being Paris's widow and the lover of ten or twelve more of Priam's sons. Hofmannsthal finds it decidedly surprising and extremely modern that in Homer Helen should speak of this terrible war and her own responsibility for it as if it had been some casual love affair after which she is homesick for Menelaus. Obviously Homer does not abide our question. His characters do not stand in any nexus of causality based on ethics. That the war was won and that Helen was recaptured are facts which he recounts. Psychological eventualities such as contempt, suspicion, remorse, or reconciliation are irrelevant to his theme.

This being so, Hofmannsthal's curiosity about Menelaus is all the more characteristic, as is his own formulation of the problem, to which he found an answer—or at least the basis of an answer—

in Euripides. Euripides described what Homer left out : the husband's return, which could now be reshaped in the light of
Hofmannsthal's particular problem of ethics. For Hofmannsthal this
problem was quite simply fidelity, a theme which he had already
dealt with in *Die Frau ohne Schatten* and, even before that, in
Christinas Heimreise, Der Abenteurer und die Sängerin, and *Der
weiße Fächer,* not to mention his earliest work, *Gestern.* Yet obviously this could not be a fidelity introduced and accounted for as
simply as Euripides manages it by means of Helen's fortunate
sojourn in her Egyptian haven. The confusion caused by the
phantom had to be spiritualized into a humanly more profound
symbol. Moreover, Hofmannsthal decided to add to the confusion
on his own account by adopting the form of a magic opera.

The charming nymph Aithra (suggested by the benevolent
prophetess Theonoe) holds the magic skein in her hand. She is well
disposed toward the somewhat bewildered royal couple of Sparta
now returning home. Hofmannsthal's decisive departure from the
myth is that the Trojan Helen actually is the real one; no Egyptian
Helen in the sense of the legend exists. Aithra saves Helen from the
sword of Menelaus by enlisting her elves to confuse his mind and
make him pursue a drift of mist which he takes for Helen. Menelaus, though, thinks that he has killed both her and Paris. Aithra
then fools Menelaus into believing that the gods gave Paris a
phantom and shows him the true Helen safe and sound in her
palace, radiant with renewed beauty. At the heart of this is the
true problem of marriage, which always contains the possibility of
unfaithfulness but is justified ethically only as infidelity reverts to
fidelity. Some lines of the fourth book of the *Odyssey* contain the
germ of Hofmannsthal's theme : original fidelity finding itself
again :

> but my heart
> sang—for I had come round, long before,
> to dreams of sailing home, and I repented
> the mad day Aphrodite
> drew me away from my dear fatherland,
> forsaking all—child, bridal bed, and husband—
> a man without defect in form or mind.[7]

Here Helen, the unfaithful, surpasses her husband in true
fidelity. He, to be sure, is plunged into greater confusion : not only

the confusion of the senses caused by Aithra's magic, but emotional confusion for which the confusion of the senses is just a symbolic metaphor. For he stands in the "situation for a husband" which inspired Hofmannsthal to rehabilitate the notorious cuckold of world literature and "to reveal the nobility and tragedy of this much ridiculed figure." The purpose of the magic symbolism in the libretto is not merely to show Helen in the genuine core of her fidelity but, more important still, to heal the disturbed soul of the loving but betrayed husband :

> Give me myself,
> my intactness,
> the boon of unriven
> manhood! Give me
> in my misfortune
> back to myself![8]

But the significant point is that the magic proves basically unnecessary; it is pushed aside; the shadow is not accepted as authentic.

In the first act recognition wavers in the bewildering magical shifts between dream and reality, and Menelaus cannot be sure that the Helen he has brought from Troy and the one who meets him in Aithra's palace are identical. In the second act, however, fidelity and the recognition of fidelity are confronted with decisions and emotions which are, so to speak, "more real." Aithra transports the couple to a "magic tent" at the foot of the Atlas Mountains, where all that is past, including all dreams and all deceptions, is to be forgotten in a new marriage :

> Behold the one who is forever yours!
> Does it not recall our wedding day?
> In its soft glow behold
> and recognize your Helen!   (p. 262)

But now the deception—the false story of the phantom—comes home to roost, and Menelaus's love, shattered as it is, breaks through in his belief that the Helen who stands before him must be the phantom siren. The memory of the Helen he believes to be real, the one who betrayed him and who he believes to be dead, takes possession of him. He goes off hunting—or wants to—in order to recapture in his giddy mind the situation when Helen was taken from him long ago :

> For when a man's been hunting
> and comes back home to his wife,
> he can never be sure
> it's the same wife he left behind!   (p. 275)

Now comes a flashback to the temptation of Helen. Here Hofmannsthal follows the Theoclymenus model but gives Helen other suitors : Altair, the mountain prince, and the boy Da-ud, a reincarnation of Paris. The gradual condensation or dissolving of magic into reality is symbolized by the fact that Menelaus, who in the first act killed a phantom Paris, now thinks in his jealousy that Paris is his victim when he is actually killing Da-ud :

> In this boy's death you hoped
> Paris of Troy would die again.   (p. 289)

But the principal symbol of this process of condensation into a reality which has to be confronted is the potion of memory, chosen in preference to the potion of forgetfulness. When Aithra tries to expunge past infidelity with the potion of forgetfulness and reunite husband and wife in shadow, not substance, Helen—opting, one might say, for a kind of Freudian therapy—finally chooses the potion of memory, that is, she chooses truth.

Both Hofmannsthal and Ernst Bloch answer the question they have raised as to the "reality" of the Trojan War and consequently the reality of its cause according to the principle of reality, although they have different conceptions of it. To Bloch the phantom of the Trojan Helen stands for the true, higher reality as opposed to the Egyptian Helen, who is real only in the literal sense. For Hofmannsthal reality is not esthetic appearance but ethical truth. The Trojan War did take place, and Helen was real and was there :

> A thousand comrades
> are waiting there.
> They came for the sake
> of Menelaus
> and Helen, his wife,
> the beautiful, the faithless.
> With rueful gestures
> complaining. . . .
> Did they die
> for a ghost?   (p. 298)

The ghost, the phantom, which in Euripides stood for Helen's rehabilitation as a faithful wife, is seen by Hofmannsthal as a deception and a masking of the truth and thus carried *ad absurdum*.
The truth is that there has been infidelity and it has reverted to
fidelity :

> Yours! Your unfaithful one
> hovering over
> the fields of repentance!   (p. 301)

While Bloch interprets the myth of the phantom and the dual
Helen as mythic symbolism, Hofmannsthal eliminates the myth.
The magic opera is almost paradoxically demythologized, revealing
a relation to its Euripidean model analogous to the relation of
Goethe's *Iphigenia* to that of Euripides. Trickery and deception,
permissible in the plays of Euripides, yield in Goethe and Hofmannsthal to truth as the only possible basis for human relationships.
Hofmannsthal's libretto, written in 1926, still belongs to the era of
humanism. It too is a "classical-romantic phantasmagoria" but a
phantasmagoria on the idea of truth, not beauty.[9]

⤳ 6 ⤶

ALCESTIS

With Helen we leave the legends of Troy and the Atridae and turn to a less vast subject, still without departing entirely from the mythic sphere into which we moved with Iphigenia and Helen. But our new topic, the Alcestis legend, has nothing to do with them, and its mythic content is of quite a different kind. The publication in 1960 of Thornton Wilder's *Alkestiade* aroused contemporary interest in this legend.[1]

The mythic element which lends it a special magic and profundity, the return of a mortal from Hades, is undoubtedly connected with the myth of Persephone, goddess of the underworld, who, having been carried off herself by Pluto, is the protector of women and who released both Alcestis and Eurydice.[2] In any case the story of Admetus, a king of Thessaly, and his wife Alcestis, daughter of King Pelias of Iolcus, is linked with the gods. Both Apollo and Hercules, the demigod, stand behind them and intervene in their existence. Let us begin with Apollo. He embarked upon a bitter feud with his father Zeus, who had killed Apollo's half-mortal son, the physician Asclepius, with a thunderbolt. In revenge Apollo killed Zeus's servants, the Cyclopes, and was punished by being forced to serve a mortal as shepherd. This mortal was Admetus of Pherae, a kind, benevolent master, for which Apollo repays him. According to prophecy, Admetus is supposed to die young. Apollo makes the Fates drunk hoping that they will forget to cut the string of Admetus' life, but has to be content with their offer to spare him if somebody else will die in his place. Admetus asks his friends, his servants, his old parents, but they all refuse. Only Alcestis, the one who is dearest to him, is willing.

All this has already happened when *Alcestis,* Euripides' earliest work, written in 438 B.C., opens.[3] As usual, a prologue, in this case spoken by Apollo himself, outlines the situation for the audience. Then Euripides goes immediately into the splendid opening scene in which Apollo tries to bargain with Thanatos (Death), to release Alcestis, whose hour has come, as the appearance of Thanatos indicates. There follows a magnificent struggle for Alcestis' life between the antagonistic powers of light and darkness, of life and death. Death, who according to his own viewpoint is in the right, rants and rages :

> You at this house, Phoebus? Why do you haunt
> the place? It is unfair to take for your own
> and spoil the death-spirits' privileges.
> Was it not enough, then, that you blocked the death
> of Admetus, and overthrew the Fates
> by a shabby wrestler's trick? And now
> your bow hand is armed to guard her too,
> Alcestis, Pelias' daughter, though she
> promised her life for her husband's.[4]

But at the very outset the audience learns that this is not to be a tragedy. Appolo warns Death that he will not triumph. The mighty hero Hercules, who can achieve the impossible, will deprive him of his victim—even though Death may not believe it and may even seem to be the victor for a time.

After this prologue come the human scenes, movingly depicted. From the chorus of old men of Pherae anxiously assembled outside the palace where Alcestis lies dying and from the old servant who tells them what is going on, we learn of the nobility of Alcestis, the love between her and Admetus, and the latter's despair. The death scene itself is enacted, with weeping children, Alcestis' farewell to her husband, and Admetus' promise to remain true to her and never to take another wife.

As preparations for the funeral are being made, Hercules arrives to pay a visit to his friends on his way to perform another feat of strength. Hercules is a wonderful, swaggering homespun character, surrounded by a divine aura yet for all that slightly burlesqued. The demigod's visit is a great honor for his host, and the hospitality motif runs parallel to the motif of sacrifice. In order not to contravene the laws of hospitality, and to keep his guest from leaving, Admetus conceals the fact that they are in mourning and tells Hercules that the funeral is that of a servant girl. He lets Hercules drink, sing, and make merry to his heart's content. In a delightful scene an old servant finally tells him what is going on. Hercules is aghast at his inappropriate behavior and deeply touched by Admetus' cultivated and considerate attitude and his regard for hospitality. He resolves to rescue Alcestis from Hades—and he succeeds. Admetus, returning from the funeral with bitter lamentations, is subjected to another test of his fidelity. Hercules leads in a veiled woman and asks if he may leave this girl in Admetus' charge until he returns. Admetus refuses, whereupon Hercules unveils Alcestis.

Such is the remarkable story of a human life permitted to exceed its allotted span—for that is certainly the most affecting aspect of the legend. But in addition to the wife's self-sacrifice and her return, this brief drama contains another motif which challenged later dramatists : Admetus' acceptance of her sacrifice. This is an unusual motif, and it appeared particularly shocking inasmuch as Admetus is not depicted as a selfish, ruthless man but as noble and sensitive, a most loving husband and a benevolent prince. Neither can it be said that Euripides simply accepted Admetus' conduct as one of the facts of the legend. In a speech by Pheres, Admetus' aged father, he at least suggests that it is questionable. Pheres himself is of course in no position to criticize his son since he, a very old man, and his aged wife would not even consider sacrificing the brief span of life remaining to them for the sake of their son's life and the happiness of his family. Father and son have a violent argument before the dead body of Alcestis, and Admetus bitterly reproaches his father with not having offered his own life. Pheres replies—with undeniable justification—that Admetus, having chosen life and left the sacrificial death to his wife, has no right to speak. He taunts his son with having found a way to become immortal by letting one wife after another die for him :

> You have found a clever scheme by which you *never* will die.
> You will always persuade the wife you have at the time
> to die for you instead.   (p. 34)

Although Euripides does at least express this view, it still does not amount to a truly integral guilt motif. If it had, the play would have turned into a tragedy. But Admetus bears no moral guilt; moreover, he punishes himself for his shortcoming—assuming that Euripides even meant it as a shortcoming—and atones for it in full measure. So long as Alcestis' death seems final, the gift of his own life is annulled by his grief, which is so overwhelming that he now wishes for death himself. The scenes of lamentation are so heart-rendingly convincing that in fact the question of guilt never poses itself, any more than do problems such as cowardice, selfishness, or lust for life, which might well arise in such a situation. The climate of this play, the human condition, is simply one of *Lebensschmerz* as such.

> Here we are in all this meaningless splendor,
> two unfortunates, who never did anything
> meriting death to offend the gods.[5]

The thought and diction of these lines make it obvious that they are not a translation of Euripides. They express precisely that idea of existential suffering that no longer raises the question of guilt and non-guilt. They occur in Hugo von Hofmannsthal's free adaptation of Euripides' *Alcestis* written in 1893, an extraordinarily profound and stylistically impressive achievement for a nineteen-year-old *Gymnasiast*. "Free adaptation" here means a totally new integument of words shaped around the existing plot; it means the elaboration and expansion of speeches, additions and omissions— in brief, small changes which on closer examination are seen to make subtle, almost imperceptible interpretive changes in the sense.

Admetus' acceptance of the sacrifice is of course retained, and it is again discussed in the scene with Pheres. But Hofmannsthal makes it even more insubstantial than Euripides by strengthening still further the noble dignity of the hospitality motif. Hercules says to the slave :

> That's really decent!
> That means much more than wine
> and guest gifts such as most kings give you.
> If manners of that sort sprouted
> in people's heads today, a lot of things

> would look a whole lot better.
> He took me in and smiled when all the time
> his heart was full of turmoil and distress.
> Knowing he's stronger, he keeps quiet
> and lets the weak man brag.   (pp. 39 ff.)

Admetus' humane nobility is here postulated as the foundation of the highest moral standards and hence of humane sociable behavior in general. But Hofmannsthal goes farther and makes Admetus aware of his responsibility, as king, to establish a moral order. This is what he means by "kingly."

> for it is my lot
> *to be so kingly* that I may forget
> all my own sorrow in that obligation.
> The young queen's lovely body is interred
> as seed under the earth. Now wondrous trees
> alive with murmuring doves will spread their boughs,
> and all the rivers of my kingdom flow
> exultantly, mirroring reflections
> of wonderfully heightened life.
> And I shall hold the reins of all this wonder,
> as now I hold this sceptre, guiding,
> controlling—and forgetting my own grief.   (p. 31)

The words *"to be so kingly,"* printed in italics, are so accentuated that they are evidently the core of Hofmannsthal's conception of Admetus—and of the Alcestis problem in general. This Admetus incorporates the sacrifice which Alcestis has made for him into the meaning and task of the life remaining to him in such a way that this sacrifice may come to represent the " seed" out of which, by way of his own sacrifice, the idea and practice of true kingship will spring in full splendor. That sacrifice consists in overcoming his own sorrow for the sake of the obligations of hospitality, which Admetus exalts to the very meaning and responsibility of kingship. In Euripides he explains and justifies his behavior only in response to the puzzled questioning of the chorus and confines his explanation to the requirements of hospitality. Hofmannsthal's Admetus does not wait to be questioned. True to himself and thereby ennobling himself, he presents his attitude as the one called for by kingship :

> Any who do not understand, who ask
> whether such conduct goes with mourning,
> any who find it heartless or inapt—
> let them be silent and remember this:
> the king did it.   (p. 30)

Here it cannot be denied that the youthful Hofmannsthal's original adaptation, imbued as it is with the stylizing flourishes of emerging *Art Nouveau,* over-elaborates the simple, human nobility of the Euripidean Admetus.

Let us turn back from Hofmannsthal's *Alcestis* modeled on Euripides to the eighteenth century and look at Wieland's operetta *Alceste,* first performed at the Weimar court theatre in 1773.[6] While this beautiful little work cannot compare with Goethe's *Iphigenie* as literature or in its world view, and while it left no particular mark on German literature, there is good reason for mentioning it in connection with *Iphigenie.* Its relation to the Greek play is analogous to the relation of Goethe's *Iphigenie* to that of Euripides, and again the connection has its roots in the age of enlightenment and humanism. In Wieland's *Alcestis* an element in the story which is felt to be archaic and incompatible with the humanistic view of man and with humanistic ethics is humanized. Just as Goethe found it impossible to let Iphigenia use trickery and deceit against Thoas, it seemed natural to Wieland to eliminate every trace of selfishness and cowardice from the character of Admetus.[7]

In this little play Admetus has no idea that Alcestis has given her life for his. The plot is changed. Admetus is ill and near death, and Alcestis asks her sister Parthenia (a character introduced for this specific purpose) to ask the Delphic oracle what his fate is to be. The answer is the traditional one : another life must be offered for his. Alcestis unhesitatingly offers her own, whereupon the illness is transferred from Admetus to Alcestis. When Admetus is told of this by Parthenia, his reaction is the natural one of the loving husband who has no wish to survive the death of his wife :

> You hope to ransom my life with your death?
> Your hope is vain! Your generosity
> is lost on me. Do not ask
> the impossible. I cannot, cannot
> outlive you. Love has intertwined

> our souls inseparably. Let them go,
> inseparably joined for ever more
> into the land of shadows.   (p. 352)

It is characteristic and entirely logical that the motif of hospitality toward Hercules, which Hofmannsthal felt obliged to heighten artificially in order to vindicate Admetus, now disappears. It is no longer needed so far as Admetus is concerned. Hercules, no longer the brash drunkard, is so moved by Alcestis' sacrifice that he sets forth without delay to rescue her from the realm of the dead. The transformation of Admetus into a completely humane and ethical figure is what called for this brief discussion of Wieland's operetta.[8]

Turning from Wieland to literature of our own time, we find several treatments of the Alcestis story, the most original and ambitious of which is Thornton Wilder's *Alcestiad*. The reason for making a direct transition from Wieland to this work written in 1955 and then going back to examine some earlier versions of the story in its light, instead of taking them up chronologically, is not merely that Wilder's work is the most significant interpretation of the theme in modern world literature; in fact this procedure arises out of the thematic problem itself. This *Alcestiad* is the richest and at the same time the most esoteric treatment of that aspect of the legend that is more meaningful problematically to the modern mind than the Admetus problem : the meaning of the sacrificial death and the return to life, that is to say, the problem of Alcestis herself.

The first difference between Wilder's *Alcestiad* and earlier versions is that he combines the traditional material with newly invented elements of action. As is nearly always the case, the contemporary work proves to be the most complex one, penetrating into obscure areas of the given subject matter which were inaccessible to earlier eras. It is Wilder's work that first brings up the truly mythic, not to say mystical element in this legend : the return of a human being from the kingdom of the dead. Here for the first time this becomes the problem and crux of the play.

The Alcestiad is written in prose but, unlike the modern French versions of Greek plays its language is not ironically modernized, being simple and neutral. The action does not hover indefinitely between classical and modern times as it does in the French plays, but is set in the time of the legend. The traditional key scenes, how-

ever, have been extended both backward and forward in time, so
that the three acts fall intentionally into trilogy form. They are
followed by a satyr play, *The Drunken Sisters,* dealing with the
earlier mythical episode of Apollo and the Fates which we mentioned at the beginning of this chapter.

The first act takes place on the day of the wedding; the second
act, twelve years later, deals with the illness of Admetus and the
sacrifice of Alcestis; the third act, another twelve years later, shows
Alcestis, after the death of Admetus, enslaved to King Agis of
Thrace, who has seized the kingdom of Thessaly.

So much for the external structure. What does it mean? It is
obvious that the story has been extended on account of Alcestis.
What is her position? She first appears on her wedding day, before
the ceremony has taken place, apparently still undecided whether
she should become the wife of Admetus. "The day of the wedding
is dawning—the greatest of all weddings, and all is *not* well in the
palace of Admetus the hospitable. . . . What keeps her from sleeping
—the princess, the bride, our future queen?" (p. 15). This is the
cry of the night watchman, one of the very poetic innovations
Wilder made in the scenic conception of this play. He relates that
several times during the night Alcestis has appeared like a sleep-
walker outside the palace and entreated Apollo for a sign. The
essential change, the reshaping and deepening of the meaning of the
story undertaken by Wilder, lies in Alcestis' relation to Apollo and
to Delphi. She has always wanted to become a priestess at Delphi.
"I want to live in reality. . .in Delphi, where truth is" (p. 20).
Delphi is the shrine of truth, of understanding, of knowledge—
knowledge of the meaning of life, which in the last analysis means
man's knowledge of himself, the "know thyself." Wilder's Alcestis is
a contemplative, introspective woman. She has never wanted to
marry, to care for a house and children. In marriage, she says,
"every day is so taken up with a thousand and one tasks, with
helping [the family] and making them comfortable, that in the
end we go to our grave loved and honored, to be sure, but as un-
knowing as the day we were born" (p. 21).

Yet if he was to write an Alcestiad at all, Wilder was obliged
to conform to the legendary model, even though his version derives
a meaning from the Greek story which it does not contain as such.
Alcestis hesitates to give her hand to Admetus in marriage because

she does not know whether this is the will of the Delphic Apollo and she is waiting for a sign from him. She receives it in the form of a dream which Admetus has had; his old nurse tells her about it. The dream was connected with the condition imposed by Alcestis that her suitors must harness a lion and a wild boar to a chariot and drive it three times around the walls of the city of Iolcus. Even Hercules, who in this version is one of the suitors, did not succeed in this, but Apollo showed Admetus in a dream how to do it. Now Alcestis understands in the bottom of her heart that her marriage to Admetus will set her on her way to Delphi. With a symbolism so subtle that it is hardly recognizable as such, Apollo's sign is not followed in the literal sense but deepened to stand for love, which alone provides a foundation for marriage and makes it possible. Love, says Admetus, enabled him to succeed where the other heroes failed. Alcestis for her part can obey her love for Admetus. Again it is obscurely suggested that she senses that love will take her by way of death to Delphi, to knowledge. "Ask me, Admetus, . . .to *live* for you as though every moment I were ready to *die* for you" (p. 44). The allusion to the Alcestis myth is quite obvious, yet at the same time these words say something that two people deeply in love are wont to say, at least in literature : that one is ready to die for the other.

Other interpretive innovations by Wilder bring the Apollo or Delphi motif into a closer, less clearly defined relationship with the sacrifice and death motif than is the case in earlier Alcestis plays. He makes use of the tradition, which actually belongs to the pre-history, to the time before the marriage, that Apollo served Admetus as a shepherd, but he gives it a new twist, making the blind prophet Tiresias (here a figure of parody) lead in four shepherds who are to serve the king. One of them is said to be Apollo, but no one will ever know which is he. During this scene, however, the god himself appears on the palace roof (or, in a variation of the stage directions, behind the characters but unseen by them). The meaning of this seems to be that Alcestis' being and her life are pervaded ever more penetratingly with the awareness of Apollo's presence. Twelve years later, however, one of the shepherds (hence possibly Apollo himself) causes the death of Admetus, having accidentally wounded the king when he was trying to settle a quarrel which had broken out among them. The wound will be mortal unless—and here the plot follows the traditional model—Alcestis dies in his place. Suggestively, she learns of this Delphic prophecy from the shepherd whose spear has wounded Admetus; before he has finished speaking she knows the truth, having known it from the outset and having desired nothing else.

The order of the Hercules scene and the rescue of Alcestis is slightly changed but their meaning is the traditional one. But now comes the third act with the post-history, which is entirely Wilder's invention. Twelve years have passed since Admetus' death, and Alcestis, now an elderly woman, is a slave in the household of King Agis of Thrace, murderer of Admetus and usurper of his throne. The plague is ravaging the country, and Alcestis, who once returned from the dead, is held responsible for bringing death upon the land. Her son, now a young man, whose life was saved in Agis' massacre, returns with a friend, seeking revenge, like Orestes. Alcestis restrains him but retribution falls upon Agis in the death of his little daughter, upon whom his life has centered. And now the low voice of Alcestis reaches him, telling him that his daughter's death will teach him the meaning of her dying so that he may apply it to his own. Agis returns to his native Thrace. But Apollo comes for Alcestis and leads her out through the gate into his grove.

The play ends with a short dialogue between the two in which Apollo tells Alcestis that for her the grave will not be the end : "You are the first of a great many who will not come to this end" (p. 113). In the prologue Apollo has already told Death that he has come to found a legend, to begin a story, and that this story will mean a change for Death. In a second conversation with him, toward the end, he says that he can only bring back from the dead those who have given their life for others. Alcestis, however, is nothing but a mortal, although Death will never take her.

We have assembled these plot elements and quotations because each of them gives a glimpse of one aspect of the meaning which Wilder extracted from the Alcestis legend. These briefly illuminated elements of meaning, precisely because they cannot be combined in a rationally explainable whole, appear to be facets of some occult meaning. Death and resurrection and the idea that only those who have died for others can be resurrected—here Wilder is bringing to light an implication of the early Alcestis legend which suggests and anticipates the mystery of Christ. His *Alcestiad* does not end with

Alcestis' first resurrection from the dead and return to earthly life. She finds true resurrection and eternal life in the grove of Apollo only after her second, final death in old age. This seems to strengthen the hint of the Christian resurrection motif, but the hint is not unequivocal nor completely fitting. Delphi, after all, is still not the Christian Heaven, the throne of God; it is the shrine of knowledge, of *gnothi seauton,* the "know thyself." Within the Greek myth, as Wilder construes it, the return of Alcestis from Hades to earthly life represents the necessary preparation for the subsequent higher stage of development, for Delphi. This preparation consists in experience of earthly death, which is a part of knowledge of life, the no longer rationally conceivable broadening of the limits which confine man and which Alcestis in her youth already longed to break through. Alcestis first meets death for the sake of someone she loves; from the outset her desire for knowledge envisaged passing through death, so that she already senses that marriage to Admetus is her road toward death. This represents a nexus of love, knowledge, and death out of which the idea of the particular human *Existenz* unfolds like a blossom : the immortality that resides in the possibility of transcending "nature," which in the Alcestis story manifests itself in death, through the higher powers of love and knowledge which set man apart from purely natural beings. This is the dominant idea of Wilder's *Alcestiad,* though it should be stressed that the particular appeal of this work is that, despite its challenge to interpretation, in the end all remains enigmatic—part of the enigma which death still represents, since we shall never know whether it is end or beginning.

Early in this century there appeared a poem which was like a faint premonition of Wilder's *Alcestiad* : Rilke's "Alcestis." In the *Neue Gedichte* of 1906 to 1907 this poem is directly preceded by the one entitled "Orpheus, Eurydice, Hermes." Both have to do with the death-problem complex of the period of the *Stundenbuch* and *Malte*; both are within the sphere of Rilke's well-known idea that death is the fruit "round which everything turns." Rilke was inevitably drawn to legends such as those of Eurydice and Alcestis, which link life and death in such a remarkable fashion. For him both characters are exceptional and exemplary in that from the very first they lived only to become ripe for death. In Rilke's poem

the Eurydice who has been set free by Persephone and brought back
by Hermes, with Orpheus leading the way, no longer turns her face
toward life :

> She thought not of the husband going before them,
> nor of the road ascending into life.
> Wrapt in herself she wandered. And her deadness
> was filling her like fullness.
> Full as a fruit with sweetness and with darkness
> was she with her great death, which was so new
> that for the time she could take nothing in.[9]

Alcestis is placed next to Eurydice. For it is characteristic that
it is only her dying that Rilke takes as his theme. The poem com-
presses the action of the play into the wedding feast, at which the
god Hermes, the messenger of death, appears :[10]

> Then all at once the Messenger was there,
> flung in among them like a new ingredient
> just as the wedding feast was boiling over.   (p. 104)

Admetus, aghast, begs and bargains "for years . . . a few days . . . for
nights, just for a single one." Although the condition that somebody
else must die in his place is never mentioned, he hastily questions
his parents, his friend. Then just the simple words : "And it was she
that came." This condensed plot seems no more than an opening
chord, an approach leading to the essential core and meaning :
Alcestis' turning toward death. She

> Speaks to the god, and the god listens to her,
> and all hear, as it were, within the god :
> None can be substitute for him. I'm that.
> I'm substitute. For no one's reached the end
> of everything as I have. What remains
> of all I used to be? What's this but dying?   (p. 106)

Nothing happens except that Alcestis follows the death god.
The rest of the legend, the illness and the appearance of Hercules,
is eliminated; Alcestis' return is at most suggested as a possibility
in the smile with which she turns back one last time :

> as radiant as a hope
> that was almost a promise: to return,
> grown up, out of the depths of death again,
> to him, the liver—   (p. 106)

This might almost be the germ of Wilder's conception. "To return, grown up, out of the depths of death" is the gist of the idea he presents : that the road to Delphi, to the holy place of knowledge, leads through the experience of death—an idea which Rilke just touches upon very guardedly in the notion of being "grown up," that is, of having attained knowledge.

Rilke's Alcestis poem is only a very faint premonition of Wilder's *Alcestiad*. A much more direct line links it to Alexander Lernet-Holenia's beautiful little playlet *Alkestis* written in 1946.[11] Word-for-word parallels suggest that this was intended as a sort of dramatic version of Rilke's poem.[12] Here again all the action is compressed into the wedding feast, which, like the behavior of the characters, is elaborated and expanded into a dramatic scene in keeping with the traditional story. The god who appears as a messenger of death and who in Rilke is more suggestive of Hermes is the traditional god of the legend, Apollo; thus when Alcestis goes toward him to give her life for Admetus the death motif is brought into a close relation with the love motif. Alcestis experiences a moment of loving union with Apollo, the god of death, as though her love for the human Admetus, for whose sake she is dying, were being replaced by love as an absolute which can be experienced only through death.

> Are you here with me? Is death, then,
> nothing else but this: that a woman
> loving a man must pass through death?
> Is it then death that surges like a spring
> inside me? For whom? Toward whom?
> A nimbus gleams to meet me; in its light
> all that I am is lost. Something tremendous
> troubles me . . . How can a girl endure this?
> God! O God!   (p. 59)

Yet death does not come as absolutely, as wordlessly as in Rilke's "Alcestis." When Apollo vanishes, ordering Alcestis to prepare and clothe herself for death, her understanding of the meaning of her dying forsakes her and she rebels again. Now another factor, a more brutal realization, occurs to her : that death means solitude. The brutal, almost tautological fact that the dying man no longer belongs to the living (described with terrifying reality in Tolstoy's

Death of Iván Ilyích) is also built into this *Alcestis* as an implication of death's meaning. Admetus has disappeared; his old parents cannot wait for their daughter-in-law to die :

> For even if we came to you
> what could we do? Death is upon you.
> Don't rely on us. We cannot help you.
> You don't belong among us any more—
> now less than ever.   (p. 65)

Alcestis must still pass through this deepest aloneness of all before she is ripe for her death, which in this play is absolute, from which there is no return, and which finally, in the second and permanent union with Apollo, is merged with the idea of absolute love. This is metaphorically represented by her apotheosis, by her "opening herself to the full" in the "immense blue light" of radiant heaven, of the heavenly city of Jerusalem, described in the words of *Revelation*, with its gates of pearl and streets of gold, into which she enters at Apollo's side. We may take the words of the heavenly choir as Lernet-Holenia's interpretation of the death motif in the Alcestis legend :

> Suffering conquers
> the unsuffering. Love conquers suffering. Deities,
> formerly mortals, already have changed the world.
> Change it again! Pass through death yourself. They too
> passed through it.   (p. 69)

Here we have an even plainer, less ambiguous allusion to the mystery of Christ than the one in Wilder's *Alcestiad*. The idea of giving one's life for another, implicit in the Greek legend, made this legend a beacon on the horizon of the Christian world.

But there have been still other interpretations of Alcestis' death and return. Ernst Wilhelm Eschmann treated them almost drastically in his play *Alkestis*, written in 1950. Its atmosphere, pervaded by the tone of common speech, seems to be the stylistic reflection of his interpretation. The action is loaded—overloaded perhaps—with characters, events, and talk; we need concern ourselves only with the underlying idea which represents a more penetrating explanation and interpretation of the Alcestis story. Here it is not Hercules' strength alone that miraculously reclaims Alcestis from death. Death, wise in his knowledge of human nature and conduct, is prevailed upon to release Alcestis from Hades not through the strength of Hercules but in response to love, the love of Admetus and his heartfelt wish.

An implication Lernet-Holenia had already associated with the death problem—the relationship of the living to their dead—here becomes the pivot of meaning of the symbolizing legend, and the scenes incorporating it are extensive. In Eschmann's version Admetus, who in the Alcestis works that are dominated by the death motif had receded more or less into the background, stands side by side with Alcestis. The happy ending of the Euripidean original takes the form of an almost bourgeois happy marriage based on love, surviving through love and symbolizing a little too neatly the mystery of love which can overcome death.[13]

_ℐ 7 ℮_

PHAEDRA

Euripides' *Alcestis,* his earliest surviving play, written in 438 B.C., was followed by *Medea* (431 B.C.) and the Phaedra tragedy which bears the name of its hero, *Hippolytus* (428 B.C.). These three plays, written so close together, are also linked thematically; they all deal with love and marriage. *Medea* and *Phaedra,* however, stand apart from *Alcestis,* not only in the tragic nature of their themes but because they have moved to a different level of artistic reality. Here the limits of human reality are not mythically transcended. If the gods play any role at all, as Aphrodite and Artemis do in *Hippolytus,* for instance, it is in the mythological, Homeric sense, as off-stage puppet masters manipulating events and lives which take place in the realm of human relations and which have psychological meaning in that realm alone. Even Medea's evil magic is not in itself mythical; it is a factor connected with her historical image and origin; its symbolic meaning remains inscrutable. What both these tragedies deal with—much more overtly than in the *Alcestis*—is the sexual relationship, archetypal situations, and problems which have existed in every era and which can be transposed into any period : woman's unrequited love, for which Phaedra is the model, and man's marital infidelity, of which *Medea* provides almost a prototype.

Although Euripides' Phaedra play is a little later chronologically than *Medea,* the thematic crescendo makes it advisable to begin with Phaedra. Euripides called the play *Hippolytus* because

117

his sympathy undoubtedly lay with the masculine member of this doomed erotic tangle. Aphrodite, goddess of love, seeks revenge against Hippolytus, son of Theseus and an Amazon, because he has scorned her, rejecting love and women to follow Artemis, the unfeminine goddess of the hunt :

> He is with her continually, this Maiden Goddess, in the greenwood.
> They hunt with hounds and clear the land of wild things.[1]

This grievous insult to her power, the mightiest force in the course of the world, is more than Aphrodite can bear. It will not go unavenged; Hippolytus must die. The means to this end is already at hand. Phaedra, Hippolytus' young stepmother, is consumed by a violent passion for him, and all Aphrodite has to do is to arrange for Theseus to discover this. The rest is inevitable, particularly after Theseus' father, Poseidon, intervenes. It brings death to Phaedra too, and although this was not Aphrodite's express intention, it does not disturb her. "Her suffering does not weigh in the scale so much / that I should let my enemies go untouched," she says coldbloodedly in the prologue, which, in Euripides' usual technique, summarizes what has gone before and what is about to happen.

Obviously Aphrodite's extremely cruel and selfish actions do not concern us here; in fact it is ultimately irrelevent that the tragedy of Phaedra and Hippolytus is engineered by a goddess. In *Hippolytus,* indeed already in *Medea,* Euripidean psychological drama comes into being, a type of drama in which the action occurs within men's minds quite independently of divine intervention, so that outward events result from inner ones. Thus it should not be overlooked that Phaedra's passion for Hippolytus is posited, quite apart from Aphrodite's plans, as an already existing ground on which Aphrodite merely builds, as the authentic, naturally given psychological situation which of itself produces what she wants to accomplish. Here lay the psychological problem : to make it plausible that Phaedra should stoop to iniquitous action.

At the very beginning of the play Phaedra's morbid love is plainly represented as a state of physical suffering. She lies on her bed, wasting away, says the chorus of women. Pursued by some secret sorrow, she longs for mournful death. The nurse—from now on always an important figure in classical love tragedies—takes the first step which will bring about her ruin. In a well-meaning attempt to help her mistress, she tells Hippolytus of Phaedra's condition, and the chaste, woman-hating youth turns upon his stepmother in a terrible outburst of rage. Her shame and humiliation at finding her love spurned produce a psychological crisis which convincingly explains her decision to end her life. Yet obviously Euripides wanted to make Phaedra inferior to Hippolytus. He therefore gives her character a streak of cowardice, of fear of Theseus and, not least, fear for her reputation. Now, she thinks, Hippolytus will betray her to Theseus and soon she will be reviled by everybody. Her own death alone will not expunge the shame in the eyes of others. She must vindicate herself, shift the blame to the one who has spurned her, and by doing so give rein to her instinctive female impulse of revenge.

What she does is devilish. She leaves a letter which Theseus, returning from heroic exploits, finds in her lifeless hand, saying that Hippolytus has violated her and profaned his father's bed. The plot draws—or rather storms—to its conclusion in a series of uncomplicated reactions. In his grief, which is movingly depicted, Theseus flies into a rage against his son, heedless of Hippolytus' assurances that the accusations are false. While he refrains from killing him, he banishes him from Athens, and Poseidon does the rest, as Aphrodite willed and foretold it. He sends a sea monster to frighten Hippolytus, who is driving his chariot wildly beside the shore. The horses bolt and his shattered body is hurled over the cliff. The *dea ex machina,* Artemis, appears too late (since this is tragedy) and informs Theseus of his son's innocence. Hippolytus is carried in, dying, and is extolled by Artemis as an eternal model of chastity. From now on brides will cut their hair in his honor the day before their marriage, and Phaedra's love for him will redound to his glory for ever.

This love tragedy is directed against Aphrodite as the goddess of love in the form of demonic passion which robs man of his dignity, and that is why Phaedra is made to act in a morally reprehensible way. Artemis and Hippolytus represent the antithesis to Phaedra, and it is significant that no other factor, such as the obvious one of the young man's homosexuality, plays any role. Hippolytus represents purely and simply the contrast between human dignity and passion, which destroys it.

The Phaedra problem, elemental but limited in range, is of interest in our present context only in the light of Robinson Jeffers' Phaedra play, *The Cretan Woman*. Fortunately, however, as we found in the case of Iphigenia, literature offers us an alternative to direct juxtaposition of the modern version and the Greek one. Instead, we can interpose and compare a third version, again a product of European classicism : Racine's famous *Phèdra*. And here again the interposition throws the relationship between the modern age and Greek antiquity into sharper profile.

The dramatist of the sophisticated cultural age of Louis XIV was obliged to mitigate the offensive character traits in both Phaedra and Hippolytus. Racine was forced to eliminate precisely the woman-hating trait that in Euripides denotes Hippolytus' virtue. Love was too central a theme of French classicism to permit the depiction of a young man completely insensitive to it. Hippolytus has to reject Phaedra's love not only because she is his father's wife but because his heart belongs to another. Racine's chaste, extremely masculine Hippolytus finds himself in love, almost against his will, with Aricie, daughter of one of Theseus' enemies. This tightens the network of psychological relationships and conflicts; Phaedra's suffering is naturally increased when she learns of his love, toward the end of the tragedy, for if Hippolytus is capable of love at all, she is doubly spurned and insulted. Phaedra also had to be made less vile than she is in Euripides, as Racine himself points out in his preface to the play. To let her make the lying accusation herself would have been too shocking to his age. Such words would be too contemptible "from the lips of a princess whose feelings are otherwise so noble and virtuous." They are more appropriate to a nurse, in whom such servile tendencies are permissible (for in classical French tragedy only people of standing were privileged to possess dignity and virtue).

The changes in the action stem from this conception. The nurse makes the false charge against Hippolytus to Theseus. The letter is eliminated, and Phaedra takes poison instead of hanging herself, so that before dying she can exonerate Hippolytus herself.[2] The important thing was to ethicize and humanize the archaic material. Classical humanism has no need of an Artemis; the deities are eliminated, Aphrodite as well as Artemis. Passion and virtue, destruction and survival, are man's affair and his alone.

More than a century later Schiller translated Racine's *Phèdre* in a version no less faithful for being in iambics. However, just as we found in the case of Iphigenia, the contemporary dramatist interested in this theme of ill-fated sexual encounter will find Euripides much closer than European classicism to the modern viewpoint. Thus a modern dramatist has been able to treat the Hippolytus problem, which Racine avoided, that is, his homosexuality, as an emotional and sexual perversion no longer to be regarded as taboo. This notion is suggested but not stressed in Euripides, being masked by Hippolytus' association with Artemis and hence with chastity.

Robinson Jeffers' *The Cretan Woman* very subtly reveals a homosexual tendency in Hippolytus. He first appears accompanied by his friends, and his favorite is explicitly described as a slender and rather effeminate young man. In Jeffers' play Hippolytus is again the real hero, a delicately organized character in whom even the homosexual tendency is aesthetically sublimated. He loves his friends "if they are brave and beautiful" and therefore shuns the chthonian realm of sexual love and procreation :

The truth is:
I am a little cold toward the divinities
That are worshipped at night, with grotesque antics; the Goddess
            of Witchcraft and the Goddess of Love. . . .
The world is full of breeders: a couple in every bush: disgusting.[3]

Thus Aphrodite, who reappears in Jeffers' play, is exalted to the cosmic, chthonian principle of love in almost the sense in which the natural philosopher Empedocles posited love as the principle of nature that unites the elements, in contradistinction to the opposing principle of hatred, which divides them.

I make the man
Lean to the woman. I make the huge blue tides of the ocean follow the
            moon; I make the multitude
Of the stars in the sky to love each other, and love the earth.
    Without my saving power
They would fly apart into the horror of night. . . .
The whole world would burst apart into smoking dust, chaos and
            darkness; all life
Would gasp and perish.   (p. 37)

Anyone who sins against this great principle of nature, the organism of life, must be punished and destroyed. And so when Aphrodite plants "the agony of love in that woman's flesh, like a poisoned sword," Phaedra herself represents something of this primal cosmic principle which is beyond good and evil. As she says to Hippolytus :

> We know that good and evil and virtue and sin—are words, tired words;
>   but *love* is more beautiful than sunrise
> Or the heart of a rose: the love of man and woman can be more beautiful
>   than the great-throated nightingale
>   Her heartbreak song.   (p. 50)

Although the Phaedra story, as we have said, is less vast and hence offers less scope for interpretation than the stories of Alcestis and Helen or the tremendous Oresteia,[4] the comparison of the contemporary Phaedra play with Euripides and with Racine reveals through its very limitations how contemporary treatments of Greek themes differ from those of earlier centuries. They do not reshape in order to humanize, but rather the reverse : they extract something that was present germinally in the Greek originals but had remained more or less amorphous, unformulated, hidden by the mythological trappings. The reason for this is probably that modern knowledge of human existence goes beyond—or, one might say, beneath—the area stamped and bounded by the classical humanistic view : beyond the conception of man as a purely spiritual and moral being. Hauptmann's Iphigenia play showed this in grandiose archaic mythological form. It emerges again on a more intimate, personal scale as the meaning of Robinson Jeffers' Phaedra play. It is almost self-evident that the Medea story holds similar potentialities.

8

MEDEA

"He knows that his name and mine are linked for the ages. Jason—
Medea! They can't be separated."[1] These are the despairing words
of Anouilh's Medea—words which express what it is that has made
this marital tragedy, first dramatized by Euripides, a perennial
tragic theme right down to the present day. Jason and Medea—
these names, linked together in enmity, set the model for the count-
less variations on the story of the faithlessly abandoned woman, a
familiar figure in real life and literature among all peoples and in
all eras. This Greek tragedy is exemplary because—not although—
it brings home to us this woman's situation in its most extreme possibilities. Even the modern and contemporary Medea plays, from
Grillparzer to Anouilh and on to Hans Henny Jahnn and Matthias
Braun, have not eliminated the extreme element : Medea's murder
of her children. In various fashions they have explored this figure,
originally established so brilliantly by Euripides; they have attempted to make Medea and her action understandable or have
raised the question whether she was entitled to such revenge.

As we all know, Medea's story rests on the Golden Fleece
legend, which originated on the wild coast of Thessaly. There a
Zeus existed who demanded the sacrifice of young boys. One of
these victims, the Greek Phrixus, whom his stepmother Ino wanted
to sacrifice, was saved through the help of Chrysomallus, the winged
golden ram, on whose back Phrixus escaped with his sister Helle
across the Black Sea. Helle fell into the sea that bears her name, the

Hellespont, but Phrixus reached Colchis, where he was taken in by King Aeëtes. In gratitude Phrixus gave the king the ram's fleece and Aeëtes set a dragon to guard it.

This legend became connected with the story of Jason and the Argonauts. Jason's uncle, Pelias of Iolcus, wishing to be rid of Jason as a claimant to his throne and hoping that the dragon will kill him, sends him to Colchis to bring back the Golden Fleece. Through her magic Aeëtes' daughter Medea helps Jason to kill the dragon. They fall in love and Medea follows him to Greece as his wife. To avenge Jason, she poisons his treacherous uncle Pelias with a magic potion and ever afterward is looked upon in Greece as an evil sorceress.

Scholars disagree whether, or to what extent, Medea is to be considered divine. The prevailing tradition says that Aeëtes was the son of Helios, so that Medea was descended from the sun god. The chariot drawn by dragons in which Euripides' Medea vanishes was sent, she herself says, by her father Helios. But according to another version of the legend, Medea was the child of Aeëtes' union with Hecate, the goddness of night and death. Wilamowitz-Moellendorff, the authority on classical philology, considered Medea an underworld goddess pure and simple and linked the name Aeëtes (by way of a controversial etymology) with Aea (earth) and hence with Hades, the "earth abyss." Medea, "daughter of the prince of Hades," is versed in the evil magic of the underworld. Wilamowitz then suggests that the daughter of Hades cannot remain on earth, that her union with a mortal cannot be successful, and that she must "descend again in horrible fashion."[2]

The pre-Argonaut tradition survives only vestigially in the *Medea* of Euripides, although he does use the vestiges in drawing Medea's character. It was he, however, who made the story into a great marital tragedy; the ghastly climax of the play, the murder of the children, was his invention. What has gone before : the Argonaut's expedition, the capture of the Golden Fleece, and Jason's liaison with Medea, is assumed to be familiar to the audience. With great artistic skill it is all recalled in a lament by the first character to appear on stage, the nurse. The audience is immediately plunged into the existing situation : Jason and Medea, having fled their country, have found refuge with King Creon of Corinth, who now wants to banish Medea and her young sons and marry

Jason to his daughter Glauce, called Creusa in many versions.

The situation existing when the play opens does not change. There is no retarding element, no peripety. The only thing that happens is that instead of sending Medea away immediately Creon grants her one night's delay—the night in which her revenge is devised and carried out. The relationship between Jason and Medea is immutable, so that all movement, all the action, internal and external, must fall to Medea, Jason being, as it were, the blank wall against which it dashes itself. Structurally, Jason's inflexible role culminates in his own self-justification, as unacceptable to the Greek mind as to ours : that having sons by the rich Greek princess whose blood is as blue as his own would benefit his sons by Medea by raising them to a position equal with that of the royal children he expects to have. He is not tired of Medea, he maintains, and he is grateful for all she has done for him, but he has repaid her fully by taking her away from her barbarian country and bringing her to civilized Greece.

> Do you think this is a bad plan?
> You wouldn't if the love question hadn't upset you.
> But you women have got into such a state of mind
> That, if your life at night is good, you think you have
> Everything; but, if in that quarter things go wrong,
> You will consider your best and truest interests
> Most hateful. It would have been better far for men
> To have got their children in some other way, and women
> Not to have existed. Then life would have been good.[3]

This really requires no commentary. None of the attempts by later dramatists to soften Jason psychologically succeeded in saving him morally or justifying him. He remains the prototype of the man who abandons his wife for the sake of material advantage and who is never at a loss for the shabbiest of excuses.

But we should see the role as one of rigid resistance, not as a wall against which Medea is shattered herself but as a wall against which the fire of her despair and revenge flares up, reducing it to rubble and ashes. If this is a metaphor, it is a concrete one suggested by the ghastly revenge she achieves. Feigning forgiveness, she sends deadly wedding gifts to the bride : a robe which clings to her body, a golden fillet from which flames spurt. Creon, throwing himself upon Creusa, dies with his daughter. Grillparzer and Anouilh make the fire destroy the castle and the whole city; in Anouilh Medea seeks her own death in it. In Euripides, however, something of her divine origin breaks through in the end. After she has killed the children, and before Jason can stab her with his sword, she appears in a chariot drawn by dragons which Helios has sent for her and vanishes from sight.

The psychological problem of Medea is neither complicated nor enigmatical. Morally she is entirely in the right. She has given all she possesses, herself and her country; for Jason's sake alone she committed crimes. Euripides made her a completely unbroken woman, driven by powerful emotions, whose love, so deeply injured and betrayed, can only turn to destructive hatred. But going beyond this, Euripides also touched upon the problems of a marriage inappropriate from the start because the partners' backgrounds and their attitude to life, mores, and morals are too different. Medea is a foreign element in Greece; to Jason, who would like to settle down there again, she is an embarrassment which he lacks the humanity, the magnanimity, and the candor to overcome. The Greek comes off badly in comparison with the barbarian. The chorus condemns him utterly. While Medea's murderous deeds are not morally extenuated, no real moral stress is placed upon them in comparison with Jason's more atrocious psychological murder of Medea. Her terrible, unnatural murder of her children is in itself the ultimate proof of how absolute her feelings are. It hurts her as much as it hurts Jason, and Euripides brings this out in her anguished monologue in which, torn by conflicting emotions, she fights her way through to the ghastly decision.

Euripides' characterization of Medea is so well motivated, so convincing, that, unlike his Iphigenia, it has never been superseded but has persisted throughout all later versions—including both Grillparzer's version and Anouilh's modern play.

Grillparzer developed Euripides' play into an epic trilogy entitled *Das Goldene Vlies* (*The Golden Fleece*), linking the Corinthian marital tragedy with the earlier love story, which provides the theme for his second play, *Die Argonauten* (*The Argonauts*), and also with the story of the Golden Fleece and the curse which falls upon all those connected with it. The subject of the Fleece is dealt with in the first play, *Der Gastfreund* (*The Guest*). So far as his characterization of Medea is concerned, these plays dealing with the prehistory serve to prepare the way psychologically for the monstrous insult and her monstrous revenge. Grillparzer tried to do this by making the love and the closeness between Jason and Medea completely real and using it as a central pivot for the colorful story of the capture of the Fleece through Medea's sorcery, and on the other hand by playing down the barbarian element to a great extent : by not making Medea guilty of the death of Pelias, for example.

This work belongs entirely to the psychologizing, historist nineteenth century; it is rich in action and motivation; its characters typify the highly developed humanity appropriate to the bourgeois, humanistic tone of the period which is so definitively dramatized in Grillparzer's work. The human relationships are more closely knit than in his Greek model. Grillparzer introduces Creusa, who does not appear in Euripides or in the contemporary modern versions, as an active character, making her delicate blonde beauty and her gentleness the personification of Greek culture and the antithesis of the dark demonic figure of Medea. Nineteenth-century drama delighted in these contrasting figures, which recall Kriemhild and Brunhild in the first plays of Hebbel's *Nibelungen,* Elsa and Ortrud in Wagner's *Lohengrin,* and a whole series of similar pairs in Ibsen.

Jason is bound in his royal relatives by the affectionate friendship of his early years, so that he is emotionally torn between the two women and his conduct is no longer purely utilitarian. Medea's psychological makeup is broadened and made softer, more susceptible to hurt and insult, by bringing in her maternal instincts. A brilliant psychological touch introduced by Grillparzer is to make the children turn away from their brutal mother toward the gentle Creusa, thus completing Medea's abandonment and isolation and making its transformation into revenge all the more convincing. This dramatist makes her a moving figure when she tries to give up her barbaric ways and, to please Jason, asks Creusa to teach her to sing and play the lyre.

These sketchy indications of Grillparzer's psychological broadening of this marital tragedy will suffice to reveal the line linking his *Medea* with the *Médée* of Anouilh, written in 1946, which develops Grillparzer's individual and personal psychologizing into a more universal and fundamental statement of the problem. At first glance the two works have nothing in common. In contrast to Grillparzer's richly orchestrated, expansive verse drama, Anouilh, as we might expect, presents us with a concise one-act play in prose, loosely divided, like the Greek tragedy (though without the chorus), into a series of dialogues between two people : Medea and the nurse, Creon and Medea, Medea and Jason, and a short concluding dialogue between Jason and the nurse. The structural climax is reached in the most extensive of the dialogue scenes, the key scene between Medea and Jason. Here something which is already perceptible in Grillparzer and even in Euripides becomes the central problem : the potentials, as typified by Medea and Jason, of an unsuitable marriage having no basis of true inner harmony. This is then expanded into the theme of the suffering which the two inflict upon one another.

In Anouilh Jason is anything but the unyielding wall against which Medea's unhappiness dashes itself. He is depicted as more sinned against than sinning—a man who was able to live with a wild and passionate nature like Medea's during his own stormy youth, but who in maturity wants order and moral discipline. The tone of the play is much the same as in Grillparzer; Anouilh's simple prose expresses the same thing that Grillparzer says in the lofty language of verse :

> I am not what I was; my strength is broken
> And courage now is dead within my breast.
> This you have done. Remembrance of the past
> Lies heavy on my troubled soul, like lead.
> I cannot lift my downcast eyes and heart.
> Besides, the youth has grown into a man,
> Outgrown his childish joy in springtime flowers,
> Wants fruit, reality, and permanence.[4]

Anouilh's Jason says the same thing in prose : "I want to be humble. I want this world, the chaos into which you led me, to take shape at last. No doubt you are right when you say that there is no reason, no light, no resting place . . . But I want to stop now and be a man" (p. 70).

Medea taunts Jason with belonging to "the race of Abel, the race of the just, the race of the rich." "It's good to have Heaven on your side and the police too, isn't it?" she asks (Anouilh, p. 71).

Behind the private problem of marriage and the sexual relationship in general, the horizon of man's life in society opens, and Jason can say with some justification : "I pity you, Medea, because you know only yourself, because you can give only to take. I pity you, chained to yourself forever in a world which you see only through your own eyes" (p. 59). Jason can say this with *some* but certainly not with absolute justification. Here is a man abandoning his once beloved wife—now an embarrassment to him—to her own chaos and seeking refuge in order. However legitimate this order may be, can such a man ever be justified?

In fact, Anouilh's *Medea* leaves this question unresolved, floating in skeptical uncertainty which one is tempted to interpret as the somewhat ironical conclusion to which, in his opinion, the ancient story of Jason and Medea leads or might well lead. For when everything has gone up in flames and smoke and Jason and the nurse are left alone on the scene of carnage, Jason heaves a sigh of relief, calls his men to watch the fire, and turns to making laws for Corinth, to establishing order and rebuilding a world free of illusions. The nurse is even more relieved. She too has something to say, namely, that after the night comes the morning, and there is the coffee to make and then the beds. She enumerates all the little daily household tasks, ending with a bit of evening gossip with the neighbours and then bed and sleep. This is something more than public order; this is the natural order of life and of daily need, which will always triumph over the suffering, disorder, and horror which men can inflict upon themselves and others. The nurse asks the guard whether there will be a good harvest this year and receives the reassuring answer that there will be enough bread for everyone. The curtain falls *while they are talking,* as the stage directions expressly state, meaning simply that life goes on and that in the importance of the harvest Medea's suffering, her crime, and her ruin will be forgotten, will sink back into the past, for only the present is life. It means too that confronted with the everlasting life of nature and the gentle rhythm of life, conflict and passion and the joys and sorrows of human existence become meaningless.

Like the Phaedra problem, the Medea problem is not particularly vast in scope. But, as we have seen, it has a tendency to expand beyond the limited theme of the problematical and tragic marriage into the individual's relationship to society, and to question his right to commit a crime against society because of what fate has done to him, however harsh and unfair. A detail worth noting is that in the more modern versions of the story the fire with which Medea intended only to kill Creusa destroys the city. Indeed the most recent Medea play pursues this line even further and more vigorously. While Matthias Braun keeps much closer to the Euripidean structure and text than Grillparzer and Anouilh did, that does not prevent him from slanting the meaning along this new line. This young writer seems to have perceived the problem posed by the *Medea* of Euripides more sharply than any of his predecessors. In a note to the acting edition of his *Medea* he asks the question : "Is *Medea* a love drama?"[5] It undoubtedly is; it is a tragedy of marriage. According to Braun's understanding of it, however, Medea's erotic situation is actually settled before the drama itself begins; as a given fact it is of course part of the drama, but the real theme of the tragedy is her subsequent situation, that is, her relationship to the world and to society. We compared Jason's attitude in Euripides to a blank wall assaulted by Medea's suffering and passion and hence related to those passions, but it is equally possible to interpret it as indicating that the marital situation is quite simply what it is, no matter how it came to be so, that it is a fact, a stage of life to which the parties involved must adjust themselves. For Medea it is an unalterable situation of the kind that may occur in any life and in any marriage. This does not excuse Jason personally, but this is no longer the point.

Braun's viewpoint explains Euripides' Jason. He underlines something already expressed by the chorus of Corinthian women in certain passages of Euripides' text : that Medea ought not to disturb the city with her personal troubles. A comparison of the two passages shows how much more intense Braun's version is. In Euripides the chorus says :

> I heard the voice, I heard the cry
> Of Colchis' wretched daughter.
> Tell me, mother, is she not yet
> At rest? Within the double gates
> Of the court I heard her cry. I am sorry
> For the sorrow of this home.   (p. 64)

Instead of rendering this passage literally, Braun heightens the meaning :

What is this? Will she never
be quiet? Will she never stop
running back and forth through the streets—
Medea—restless and ranting,
startling us out of the shade of our rooms
as she goes about dragging from door to door
her inexhaustible load of complaints,
seeking women to help her bear an exorbitant woe?   (p. 75)

"Exorbitant woe"—this is, in the last analysis, Braun's pregnant formulation of the problem of Euripides' Medea. Who could deny that she is pitiful and truly deserving of sympathy? But many people are pitiful, some in one way, some in another. Does this give them the right to bother others with their personal troubles? Braun expressly refers to Medea's inexhaustible load of "complaints," not of trouble.

This dramatist brings out the relationship between personal concerns and the common interest even more strongly than Euripides or even Anouilh did, by pointing to conditions in the city. The political situation both at home and abroad is in any case precarious enough :

All around are troubles and feuds enough, rulers
at odds, greedy and bellicose, watchfully waiting
for chaos in Corinth and
for the city, weakened, to fall a prey to all
who are ready to batten on it.   (p. 81)

Internal disorder is the last thing they need, and Medea, who is not just anyone but a connection of the royal house, which she is disturbing and threatening with her personal affairs, is already a cause of potential danger—"simply because you are uncontrolled," as the women reproachfully tell her.

Through another innovation, or rather by giving a new twist to a character who appears in Euripides, Braun projects the Medea story still further into political and social problems. This character is King Aegeus of Athens, whom the more modern versions of the tragedy had eliminated.[6] He is a guest, a friend, of Creon of Corinth and in the Greek play is about to leave the city when he meets Medea, to whom he is sympathetic. He offers her refuge in Athens if she is forced to leave Corinth. He also bewails his childless marriage, and Medea promises to remedy this by her magic. Later dramatists found this figure superfluous and irrelevant to the action. Braun, however, makes use of it and incorporates King Aegeus, completely recast of course, into the meaning of the Medea story. He exploits the possibility that Euripides intended Aegeus' grief at being childless to offer a contrast to Medea's murder of her children, and he does it by letting the king enter bearing the body of his son, who has been killed in the fighting for the city. This serves two purposes. First, at the sight of this grief-stricken man Medea suddenly realizes what it means to have no children :

> Wait, man, tell me again what it is
> to be without sons. Show me again
> in your face, before you go away, this horror
> which you feel at the death of sons.
> I need to see it. I want to remember
> that look in the eyes of a man
> to whom they have done that.   (p. 113)

Secondly, the death of this young fighter and beloved son prompts a lament by his father which, instead of inveighing against war for demanding such sacrifices, ruefully considers man's situation : needing the state and being forced to defend it by killing and being killed. "For killing enemies is killing, too."

> Many a good man is murdered then
> and done to death. Like my child here.
> Although abiding by principles of humanity
> and even defending them, some
> get dragged into things inhuman.   (p. 111)

The father's lament over the insufficiencies of the world which man has created ends with the humane, self-transcending thought that "even as we bend over this body," we cannot stop thinking about "that which is so sorely lacking in us : man's goodness"—even though hatred comes more naturally to us when we view the evil which men inflict upon one another.

In this Aegeus, Braun has presented a destiny, a human lot, intended to provide a contrast to Medea's and to accentuate her selfishness and destructiveness, which harp incessantly upon her own grievance. This is the destructiveness of one who wants to make others suffer just because he is suffering himself :

But you shall stand out in the open,
defenseless, because, you see, that is the way I stood.
and your voice will be shouted down
and it will not be heard,
any more than my voice was heard.   (p. 115)

Thus Braun's *Medea* is no longer merely the tragedy of the
faithlessly abandoned wife or the marital tragedy of two unsuited
partners; it is here subordinated to the ethical question whether
man has the right to take disruptive and destructive action against
society on account of an injustive done to him. Braun's Medea is
not destroyed physically, as Anouilh's is. In accordance with the
Euripidean tradition she vanishes, goes away. No judgment is
passed; the question is simply posed, and the audience is challenged
to think about the relationship and distribution of suffering and
guilt in this particular case. While this aspect of the play is derived
from Euripides, it is eclipsed in the Greek play by the marital
tragedy. Nonetheless it already exists even there as a latent
possibility.

Despite all the variations, the spiritual and ethical problem of
Medea's situation follows a discernible line from Grillparzer through
Anouilh down to Braun. For this reason the constellation of characters has remained essentially unchanged. In 1926, however, Hans
Henny Jahnn, the North German novelist and dramatist, organ
builder and hormone research chemist, published a *Medea* which
diverges from this line. By radically altering the action, this writer,
who likes to explore extreme emotional drives, reduces the Medea
theme to her own terribly disturbed sexuality. In order to dramatize
this rejected woman's ruthlessly exposed bodily desires as the core
of her suffering, he presents her as an aging woman :

> You are not old!
> I am the one that's old. Were you, like me,
> close to the grave, passion
> would not be driving you away from me. . . .
> This I complain about, not your strength,
> which like a torrent overflows its banks,
> but that I am abandoned, like a dried up sea,
> denied even a few paltry drops,
> although already parched to salty ridges.[7]

In a certain sense the word "disgusting" used by Jeffers' Hippolytus applies to the sexual atmosphere of this play. It is underlined by the change which Jahnn makes in the murder of the children and in the children themselves. The sons are grown youths, especially the older one, who is passionately in love with Creusa, here depicted as an Amazon if not an outright vamp. Jason's guilt is thus sharpened because he is his own son's rival, while at the same time Medea's maternal sorrow over her son's destroyed happiness weights the scale against Jason. Yet when the sexual aspect or complex of love and marriage comes to stand so exclusively for love and marriage themselves, the danger of perversion is imminent. Medea's decision to kill the boys is a perversion inasmuch as the image of her son's frustrated union with Creusa has played a part in it—for to see this union consummated would have been a vicarious satisfaction for her. Also perverted is Jahnn's idea of making the son in his violent anguish clutch his young brother lasciviously, so that Medea must pierce the intertwined bodies in her terrible ecstasy of killing. One balks at paraphrasing her own description of this act.

When we used the word "danger" in connection with this perversion, the extreme climax of the sexual problem (which also seeks expression in the diction of this verse play) we intended no literary value judgment but at most a judgment of taste. So far as the Medea model and the Medea theme are concerned, the figure of this untamed, explosively passionate woman, who expends herself totally in love and hatred, allows us to single out the primitive sexual stratum as the most sensitive exposed nerve of her rejection. Jeffers dealt with the Phaedra theme in a similar, though gentler and perhaps more poetic way. In his case a modern dehumanized conception, influenced by archaeology and research into sexuality, was able to bring to light those archaic sides of Greek art and literature that were inaccessible to European classicism. Jahnn has exposed them again in Medea's suffering, with all the brutality inherent in this model of feminine revenge which has served as an extreme example ever since Euripides.

⎯ 9 ⎯
OEDIPUS

It seems odd that the mightiest figure in Greek tragedy should contribute much less to our present theme than the characters so far discussed, and less even than Antigone. The modern successors of Sophocles' *Oedipus the King,* from Corneille and Voltaire down to Gide and Cocteau, fail, fade, and vanish by contrast with this supreme tragedy of Greek classicism. The major reason for this may be the very perfection of this model of analytical disclosure technique, but there seem to be other reasons inherent in the subject itself.

This story is something quite different from the Oresteia or even from a subject which leads into myth, as the Alcestis story does, not to mention the tragedies of Phaedra and Medea. Here we are not dealing with the archaic or mythical events of a subject from classical antiquity. The range of Greek themes in world dramatic literature shows that wholly modern versions have been able to absorb elements of this kind and use them in widely diverse ways. For even within the events of specific archaic or mythic tradition, the situations are always ones in which men act or are forced to act, so that dramatists of different epochs have had considerable scope in handling the problems and conceiving the characters. The situation of Oedipus offers no such scope for interpretation. To an extent unequalled in any of the plays we have examined so far, it is an event in the most pregnant sense of the word. And there is only one single element of activity to correspond to that happening :

135

the king's search and questioning to uncover the truth of what has occurred.

Any conceivable version of the Sophoclean tragedy must retain unchanged the facts of past events if it is to be an Oedipus version at all. The facts are these : first, the two interventions of the Delphic oracle, which compels those it addresses to fulfill the prophecy through their very efforts to escape it. Laius and Jocasta fulfill it by giving their newborn son, destined to murder his father, to a servant to be killed; Oedipus fulfills it by leaving the home of his supposed parents because Delphi has prophesied that he will kill his father and marry his mother. The second fact is the murder of Laius at the crossroads, and the third the marriage of Oedipus to the widowed queen of Thebes, Jocasta, after he has vanquished the Sphinx. Such are the well known events of the past; they are supplemented by two more which set in motion the drama of disclosure : the plague and the third Delphic oracle, which says that the still unavenged murder of Laius is to blame for it.

These past events differ from the prehistory of, say, the *Oresteia* in that they involve no moral crimes that demand expiation and drive men to distraction. On the contrary, were they to remain undisclosed, men's lives would continue undisturbed, not only externally but in the deeper sense that what has occurred would be nothing more than occurrences, chance, enigmatic events. Although outwardly these events might be crimes, in the ethical sense they would not, having been committed unknowingly. Oedipus, who kills his father, is not guilty of parricide in the sense in which Clytemnestra is guilty of the murder of her husband. The marriage of Jocasta and Oedipus does not incur the odium of incest because incestuous desires were not involved.

For the purposes of our thesis we can ignore the interpretation that Sophocles obviously intended : that however powerful, clever, and wise man may seem, his power and knowledge are limited. The famous choral ode from *Antigone,* "There are many wonders in the world, but nothing is more wonderful than man," recognizes death as man's limitation, thus reiterating this interpretation of life. *Oedipus the King* might indeed almost be considered an even plainer restatement of this ode than the *Antigone* itself. Here, however, the given fact of the events themselves, past and present, is more important than any interpretation of them. Their dramatic nature and effect are not intrinsic but come from the suspense attached to their disclosure. This already provides one explanation for the failure of the Oedipus story to inspire later versions of it. Sophocles' technique of disclosure cannot be surpassed; this is what gives this tragedy its power. Unlike the *Oresteia* or Sophocles' other great work, *Antigone, Oedipus the King* provides no possibilities of interpreting an action, a conflict, or a decision determined by the character of the person who makes it.[1]

This brings us to the second element, which in a way counterbalances the passive nature of past events : the activity of Oedipus himself. For the dramatic forcefulness of the process of disclosure is closely connected with the king's prompt and vigorous inquiring and questioning once he receives the message from Delphi that the murderer of Laius has never been caught. This tragedy owes its wonderful cohesive unity to the fact that the process of disclosure reveals the character of Oedipus : a man quick to make up his mind and to act, courageous, absolute, and unsparing of himself in his determination to discover the obscure truth which, once revealed, will destroy his happiness and his very life.[2] Oedipus is the most absolute of all Sophocles' absolute characters, because, unlike the others (Electra and Antigone, for instance, who are carrying out a divinely imposed family duty) he is concerned solely with truth— a truth which, undisclosed, as Tiresias and Jocasta would like it to remain, would leave life and happiness intact. It may be objected that within the structural context of this play the revelation of the truth, that is, the identification of the murderer of Laius, is the condition upon which the city's deliverance from the plague depends, so that Oedipus is obliged to discover the truth for the sake of Thebes. But it is clear that once Oedipus has begun his questioning it is not for this reason that he pursues it and that the only function of the plague in the dramatic structure is to set in motion his quest for the truth. The fate of Thebes is forgotten when in the end Jocasta hangs herself and Oedipus puts out his eyes. This action, going beyond the penalty of banishment which Oedipus had decreed for the murderer, is a self-mutilation and hence an existential self-destruction in which the absoluteness of his nature is realized in its most extreme form.

The two structural elements from which this tautly knit play is constructed—an action in which accidents cumulate to become destiny, and the absoluteness of Oedipus, who does not evade destiny once it has shown its hand—coincide so as to leave little scope for adaptations that might draw from or add to interpretations of the story going beyond the Sophoclean model. In the few cases where this does occur, the scope has been widened by introducing a variety of elements. This distorts the Oedipus model in a manner quite different from what happens in the adaptations of any other Greek tragedy, so that the tremendous events, unequalled in world literature in their power to arouse "terror and pity," become almost a matter of indifference. This applies to the Oedipus plays of Corneille and Racine, both of which are inferior (and for good reason) to their masterworks, as it applies to the modern prose versions by Gide and Cocteau. (Cocteau's play, which confines itself to dissolving the original form into everyday speech, does not expand the thematic or problematic range at all.)

The French classicists expand the play with the love conflicts which they are so reluctant to relinquish. Disregarding chronology for thematic and methodological reasons, let us take Voltaire first. His *Oedipe*, written in 1718, still concentrates on the royal couple, inventing an earlier love between Jocasta and Philoctetes, prince of Euboea, to explain why Jocasta does not love Oedipus with true passion. A rationalist like Voltaire needed a clear-cut reason for calling the union unnatural; he was not content to depict a naturally repugnant feeling (as even his great contemporary of the Enlightenment, Lessing, does in the story of Recha and her brother, the Templar, in *Nathan der Weise*). Yet he develops the Oedipus story independently of Jocasta's relationship to Philoctetes, and this formal characteristic is in itself a sign of the weakness of the play, in which interest centers more on Jocasta than on Oedipus.

Corneille in his *Oedipe* (1659) invented an even more extended and complicated plot in which mundane family conflicts culminate in catastrophe, although here again no causal connection exists. A daughter of Laius and Jocasta (the sister of Oedipus) living at his court regards her mother's second husband as something of a usurper. Her determination to marry the young Theseus meets with the opposition of her stepfather, who had intended him for his daughter Antigone. Oracles and the arrival of the messenger from Corinth do indeed precipitate the catastrophe, but the Oedipus story recedes into the background simply because the prophecies are minimized and thus do not express the tragic situation in which every step Oedipus takes to avoid his fate brings it closer. When the curtain falls the happy couple holds the stage.

These weak and deviant adaptations by the classical French dramatists have been briefly examined because they expose very plainly the risks which reworkings of the Oedipus story incur when they expand it by introducing purely external elements and thereby ruin it.

It goes without saying that the modern French writer André Gide did not attempt to broaden the thematic range in this compact manner. He confines himself more or less to the familiar characters of the legend, taking the minor liberty of assembling certain members of the family who, if they appear at all in Sophocles, do so only as children (Antigone and Ismene, for instance) or in non-speaking roles. As a result this play too is a family portrait. Gide also yields to the tendency of modern French adaptors of Greek themes to de-historicize ancient happenings, through modern patterns of thought and speech, into potential contemporary events or at least into timeless ones, which could occur in any age. In Anouilh's *Antigone,* as we shall see, this process coincides in a certain sense with the reshaping of a Greek element of meaning into a modern one. The reason this modern version cannot hold its own against the Greek one seems again to lie in the strict limitation of the Oedipus theme.

Gide sets the tragic happening within the family, indeed within the common round of daily family life. Creon, the uncle, worries about the nervous state of Ismene, the lover of life. Tiresias has been turned into a bourgeois tutor who has a strong influence on the pious Antigone. The sons Polynices and Eteocles even harbor incestuous desires toward their sister. Gide is trying to produce the atmosphere of a distinctly human, not to say bourgeois milieu which is very far removed from a world still dominated by gods and divine commands. Here Delphi is hardly consulted; the oracle carries little weight : "The oracles are good for the common people but they don't impress us."[3] Above all—and this is a key factor in Gide's conception—he eliminates the crucial prophecy in the prehistory : that Oedipus will murder his father and marry his mother. On his way to Delphi to ask the oracle about his birth Oedipus has been turned back on the grounds that he cannot approach an altar with hands stained with murder—as they are indeed stained, because the killing of Laius at the crossroads now takes place before the journey to Delphi. This means that quite apart from the dramatic and tragic unfolding of the Sophoclean tragedy, the perfect integration of the process of disclosure with Oedipus' character no longer exists.

Gide's Oedipus is by no means unlike Sartre's Orestes in conception. It is not by chance that the motto prefixed to the first act is the choral line from Sophocles' *Antigone*, "Nothing is more wonderful thàn man," and that the answer to the riddle of the Sphinx— "Man"—is symptomatically stressed (p. 283). The basis of Oedipus' character is the pride, the strength, and the power which being a man entails, and he admits that it was from his illegitimate birth that he got that pride in owing the glory he has attained to nobody but himself. "A lost child, a foundling, possessing no civil status, no identity papers, I am particularly glad that I owe it all to myself alone" (p. 253). (Whether or not Gide used a dubious version of the legend, in which Oedipus knows from the outset that he is a foundling, is irrelevant.) The vital point of Sophocles' *Oedipus the King* has been eliminated : that to evade fate is to bring it to pass, that there is a limit to man's knowing and willing. Oedipus himself guesses and knows the truth, without having to question messengers and shepherds.

Although Gide did not completely recast his material, as Sartre did, but retained Jocasta's suicide, the blinding and the leaving of the city, these events are stripped of their awe-inspiring power. Creon can say : "I am glad to see that your pain is on the whole bearable, my dear Oedipus" (p. 301), so that he can without qualm give his brother-in-law the unfortunate news that he must leave Thebes. The terrible happening is stripped of its "terror." While in Sophocles the question of man's greatness and smallness merely arises out of the event, in Gide it is discussed in explicit speeches and dialogues and resolved in favor of man and against destiny— and ultimately against piety and belief in the gods.

Hofmannsthal's ambitious verse play *Ödipus und die Sphinx* (1905) stands outside the specific Oedipus problem complex, and this is why we are dealing with it separately and out of chronological context, following the discussion of Gide's *Oedipus*, which was written much later, in 1930. Since the action of Hofmannsthal's play is set in the period preceding the traditional main action, in its prehistory, between the consulting of the oracle by Oedipus and his winning of Jocasta in marriage, the Sophoclean model situation does not exist here. In world literature, in fact, the character which Sophocles first established has been reduced to what one might call a "prefigure." Seen in this way, Hofmannsthal's Oedipus is analogous to Hauptmann's Delphic Iphigenia, except that the latter (who in comparison with the Iphigenia of literary tradition might be called a "post-figure") is drawn from elements in the legend not previously used in the familiar Iphigenia plays, whereas Hofmannsthal builds upon the mythical tradition which in the Oedipus tragedies appears as prehistory. But this comparison of subject matter discloses another difference, this time in dramatic content, connected with the same "pre" and "post" concept. If we disregard the poetic quality of the diction, where Hofmannsthal unquestionably excells Hauptmann, the latter's concept must be considered far more successful. His reshaping of Iphigenia drew upon hitherto unknown legendary material; moreover, it did not clash with any existing Iphigenia play—any more than his subsequent versions of the Oedipus, Orestes, and Antigone themes clashed with the standard versions, whatever we may think of them otherwise.

The problem here is not one of quality or innovations and additions intended to broaden and reshape the theme, but one of fundamental concepts. Hofmannsthal's conception of Oedipus is unfortunate, in fact almost untenable. The prefigure to Sophocles' Oedipus—and that means to the Oedipus situation, which is identical with his character—appears inaptly conceived, even when we bear in mind that *Oedipus and the Sphinx* was intended to be the first play of a trilogy of which the second was to be Hofmannsthal's already existing adaptation of Sophocles' *Oedipus the King* and the final one an *Oedipus at Colonus* also modeled on Sophocles' last play. Our only concern here, however, is with the fact that there *is* an *Oedipus Rex* by Sophocles, for the existence of this play renders the expansion of its prehistory into a separate work dubious, to say the least, as we shall briefly show.

The first act presents Oedipus ready to leave his parents' house at Corinth after having learned of the Delphic prophecy. Here we encounter a passage—a key passage—which already embodies the difficulty of the whole conception (and we must emphasize the skill-ful construction of this act, which admirably develops the desperate situation and character of the young Oedipus through a dialogue with the old servant Phoenix, who wants him to return). It is the very wording of the oracle, as Oedipus recounts it, that contains the germ of this problematical conception :

> Upon your father
> You have indulged your killer's lust,
> your lover's lust upon your mother.
> This has been dreamed and this will come to pass.[4]

Though stated as a dream induced by the priestess at Delphi, the coming events are predicted simultaneously in the perfect tense, the tense of things past, and in the tense of things to come, the future. The horizon of becoming, the future, is simultaneously opened and closed. When the situation that Sophocles presents in *Oedipus the King* as an existential condition, breaking open the abyss of past events, is presented in a still emergent state, the Oedipus destiny is doubly nullified or devalued in its own inescap-able fulfillment : both in the drama of the prehistory taken by itself and also in its relationship to the revelation still to come, that is, the Oedipus drama proper. In the first case the disclosure remains in doubt, the state of not knowing might appear permanent, the oracle unfulfilled, whereas in the second case, the dramatized prehistory represents a repetition of the drama of disclosure in which this pre-history, implicit in the theme, is identical with the disclosure.

This looks, to be sure, like a too-dialectically structured analysis which overlooks the richly orchestrated theme of Hofmannsthal's work. But it points up the weak spot of the conception precisely in order to reveal the dramatist's effort to master the difficulty of depicting this prefigure. It is no accident that the play gets its title from the Sphinx scene in the last act. We believe we can show that the obscurity of this scene is directly related to the problems inherent in this conception.

In the legend the prize for vanquishing the Sphinx is the hand of the queen, whom Oedipus has not met. For reasons inherent in his Oedipus conception, Hofmannsthal places the meeting with Jocasta before the struggle with the Sphinx, since this is the moment when they fall in love—a love which in Jocasta already seems to rise from the unconscious ground of her maternal relationship to Oedipus. "Laius!" she cries when she first sees him, and in her first speech the key word "mother" occurs twice. The tenebrous, chthonian, erotic ground of life, the elemental principle of motherhood, in which this tragedy of the pre-Oedipus is embedded, is of the essence. One might say that within this Sophoclean Oedipus situation it is the incest, the sexual, erotic event itself, that has become decisive for Hofmannsthal. Oedipus as his mother's husband—this is the true tragic situation, compared to which the parricide recedes into the background, as does the disclosure itself, together with any interpretation that can be attached to it : destiny, the realization of the appearance of existence, and so on.

The erotic life and desires of Hofmannsthal's young Oedipus are dominated by a mother image before he ever sees Jocasta. The image of the woman he believes to be his mother, Merope of Corinth, has lain forbiddingly "like a sword" on the threshold of every bridal chamber—a model in perhaps even a natural sense :

> I had seen in my own mother how queens walk. . . .
> And I knew: some day I shall beget children upon one
> who with sanctified hands in the dusky grove
> may perform rites forbidden to all but her.   (p. 298)

But image and realization fantasies merge into one, into the compulsion, the longing, to sink into the maternal womb :

> Children I shall beget in so sacred a womb
> or I'll die childless.   (p. 299)

In a tragic, ironic dialectic, the attempt of Oedipus to flee the maternal womb after he hears the prophecy leads him to it—from the mother image to the mother herself. The conception of *Oedipus and the Sphinx* can be interpreted to mean that what Sophocles' *Oedipus the King* presents as the universal human destiny of tragic error has been condensed and shifted downward into the chthonian nether region of life, of sex, of generation, where the mother principles rules and is sacred :

> Yet the mothers—to the mother—
> the mothers draw everything after them.
> The blood is strong; the world rests on the mothers.   (p. 364)

The mother principle has not yet been differentiated, so to speak, into the taboo of incest, so that husband and son can be one and the same—the child-begetting "god" whom the old queen Antiope, mother of Laius, sees approaching the young widowed Jocasta. But Tiresias, the blind seer, who announces his approach, throws himself down before Jocasta, the "mother," being consecrated by her, not she by him, the priest : "No, mother, it is you who make me holy" (p. 377).

For good reason the mother principle becomes the theme of the wonderful scene between Jocasta and Antiope in the middle act. They are the mothers; their talk is of fertility. Antiope, boasting of her lost fertility, is hostile to Jocasta, whom she believes to be barren. It is characteristic enough that when she has learned the truth of the prophecy and of the son exposed long ago, she immediately sees Jocasta as a woman radiant with approaching motherhood and recognizes the coming of

> the god who is to marry you
> and call to life for Laius, Laius dead,
> an heir out of your womb. (p. 360)

We cannot tell definitely from the play whether or in what sense the defeat of the Sphinx is related to the incest motif, the chthonian realm. Since the play is entitled *Oedipus and the Sphinx,* the encounter with the Sphinx must, or should, have a key significance. This is to disregard Creon, who is drawn into the scene with the Sphinx and plays an important though overextended part, less in the development of the plot than as a character, as a counter-image to Oedipus, and as the unsuccessful, jealous contender for the throne. He accompanies Oedipus to the rock of the Sphinx in the hope of seeing him defeated and killed, but remains to bow before the victor, whom he now takes for a god. Hofmannsthal wanted to present the riddle of the Sphinx as a riddle. The answer to it, the word "man," is never given. The Sphinx retreats before Oedipus as if, or because, she recognizes him, and hurls herself into the abyss. But when Oedipus experiences this terrible spectacle, the eye-to-eye encounter with the demon, like a death blow and believes that he cannot go on living, it is as if recognition by the Sphinx were identical with his recognizing himself—his own demon, in confirmation of the Delphic dream :

> Kill me then! Can you not tell that I
> am laden with curses, flecked with evil
> like a panther's hide! (p. 405)

But his demon is the fulfilment of the prophetic dream, the attaining of supreme happiness and supreme suffering :

> I could believe that I tonight performed
> the deed which from the flickering fields of Heaven
> with sacred hand snatches the bloom of life.
> I could believe I am the greatest of all men,
> good fortune's favorite son. Here, take it!
> Quick! Kill me now! (p. 405)

The play ends with the union with Jocasta, supreme happiness, and rebirth to new—and true—life. This ending is the happy ending which terminates the prehistory, presented without any allusion to the audience's awareness of the future with which it is pregnant. Alternatively, this ending is one of tragic irony, since Hofmannsthal, like the Greek tragedians, can count on his audience's being familiar with the story and knowing more about the hero than he knows himself. Yet the classical constellation cannot simply be applied to modern drama and modern audiences. If in the bliss of the union with Jocasta the forthcoming catastrophe shows through, even without reference to what is going to happen (the Sophoclean Oedipus situation), if indeed this bliss not only contains but *is* this catastrophe, the reason is to be found, within the structure of the drama, in the preceding encounter with the Sphinx, which has been as terrible as it has been darkly mysterious, producing a death wish rather than a wish to live. This encounter looms behind the foreground of blissful union like a dark ground and an abyss; it is visible through this foreground, and even without foreknowledge of what will come to pass, it turns the happy ending of the drama into tragedy. Only in this way do this scene and the title *Oedipus and the Sphinx* reveal their function in the play as a whole.

This analysis and interpretation of Hofmannsthal's Oedipus play seem to disprove our contention about the difficulties and precariousness inherent in conceiving the Oedipus figure as a pre-figure for *Oedipus the King,* and to vindicate the play against that criticism. We must, however, keep in mind that it was precisely the obscurity of the Sphinx scene that in our interpretation shed light on the meaning of the play, so to speak. Taken by itself, the Sphinx scene is not understandable, and we have to grant that it is meant to be enigmatic. But this, precisely, constitutes the artistic problem complex to be considered in judging the structure of the drama. Within the construction of the project as a whole, the enigmatic nature of the Sphinx scene has to provide for the fatality inherent in the union between Oedipus and Jocasta, who will recognize each other as son and mother only in the "future," namely, in a second play, speaking from the literary viewpoint; this would then make the play of recognition and discovery a repetition of what is already known from the first play. In this peculiar and indeed somewhat indirect fashion even the great and poetically outstanding work of Hofmannsthal points once more to the limited scope which the specific Oedipus theme offers for variation.

⚜ 10 ⚜

ANTIGONE

One reason for presenting Antigone last in our analysis of the figures of Greek tragedy is that the story of this famous daughter of Oedipus follows his and that she, like him, was established in literature for all time by Sophocles. But over and above this, the unique nature of the Antigone theme and its literary constellation makes it particularly well suited to add a forceful finishing touch to our thesis.

Let us look first at the Sophoclean tragedy. The play and its interpretations are obviously a special case. Nothing, it seems could be more monolithic and understandable than the plot, the heroine, the conflict, and the problem of Sophocles' *Antigone*. It is therefore all the more surprising that ever since Goethe, Hölderlin, and Hegel, almost no Greek tragedy has been more frequently and contra-dictorily interpreted than this one. Karl Reinhardt could even say in his fine book on Sophocles that one can only conclude, in view of "such numerous and contradictory attempts to characterize and categorize the figure of Antigone. . .that there is in fact something enigmatic in her, something beyond comprehension—and not only to Creon."[1]

Yet the traditional literary view has seen Antigone's nature and conflict as clear and straightforward rather than enigmatic. She upholds, against her uncle Creon, King of Thebes, the unwritten divine law which requires her to bury her brother Polynices, who Creon has decreed is to remain unburied for having attacked his

147

native city. But their brother Eteocles, ruler of Thebes since the death of Oedipus (who has been killed in single combat with Polynices) is given a state funeral as defender of the city.

Like all Sophoclean heroes and heroines, Antigone acts absolutely. She accepts death, the penalty for disobeying the king's decree :

> But all your strength is weakness itself against
> The immortal unrecorded laws of God.
> They are not merely now: they were, and shall be,
> Operative for ever, beyond man utterly.[2]

Not for the sake of any man-made law, she says, will she incur the punishment of the gods. The explanation of this has always seemed straightforward enough; there are apparently no textual obscurities to complicate it. Antigone's right, the duty required by love for her dead brother, triumphs over Creon's right, which he defends against the arguments of his son Haemon, Antigone's future husband, as constitutional right, maintaining that to make an exception for a relative would be an infraction of the justice he is bound to exercise as king, and hence of the order of the state :

> Of all the people in this city, only she
> has had contempt for my law and broken it.
> Do you want me to show myself weak before the people?
> Or to break my sworn word? No, and I will not.
> The woman dies. . . .
>
> Show me the man who keeps his house in hand,
> He's fit for public authority. . . .
>
> Whoever is chosen to govern should be obeyed—
> Must be obeyed, in all things, great and small,
> Just and unjust! . . .
>
> Anarchy! Anarchy! Show me a greater evil!   (pp. 211–212)

Yet when Creon's eyes are opened by Tiresias to his injustice and he is himself threatened with misfortune if he puts Antigone to death, he decides to save her. But it is too late. She has already hanged herself in the vault; at her feet Haemon drives his own sword into his side. Creon remains, beaten, terribly in the wrong, defeated by Antigone in death.

Hegel, who called *Antigone* "the most excellent, the most

satisfying work of art among all the splendors of the ancient and the modern world,"[3] did not, to be sure, find it satisfying because of the absolute victory of Antigone's right. For him both Antigone and Creon personify moral forces which have come into conflict with one another : love of family and the rights of the state. Both are destroyed (Creon not physically but through the loss of his happiness), but they are destroyed only as individuals. Their ideas do not perish, but only the individuals who represent them, and they perish because they both represent only one side of the idea of eternal justice. Both of them are right and both of them are wrong, because both of them are right only one-sidedly. "It is only against one-sidedness that justice is aroused," says Hegel.[4] One can of course raise the objection that even if he is right and Sophocles' tragedy does contain such a complicated philosophy of justice, Creon should still not give in and flout constitutional law when Tiresias threatens him with misfortune. If the state is more important to him than family love and his personal destiny, he should accept the consequences which Tiresias warns him will ensue from his actions toward Polynices and Antigone. But he tries to ward them off, to save Antigone at the last minute, to exempt her from the constitutional law he represents, so that Hegel's interpretation is not even consistent with the action. Other scholars, for instance Heinrich Weinstock, put Creon in the wrong because his concept of the state lacks piety and is unrelated to the divine, whereas Antigone bases her claim upon the gods of the underworld who dictate her acts.[5]

However the critics may allocate the right and wrong between Antigone and Creon, Wolfgang Schadewaldt summed up the position when he said that the meaning of the work is ultimately a *metabasis eis allo genos,* that it moves into a sphere alien to the work, so that no rational interpretation, however well it fits, can encompass it. He makes this statement in an introduction to Orff's setting of Hölderlin's translation of the *Antigone* and remarks that it is a good thing that another mode of interpretation exists besides conceptual thinking—in this case music, which enters into a mystical unity with the flesh of the word in a way which cannot easily be explained.[6]

In the case of *Antigone* there exists—perhaps through an accident of literary history, perhaps not—an interpretive work which in a certain sense stands between the abstract explanations of the literary critics and the philosophers and music, which arouses only an intuitive response. This is a work of literature : the *Antigone* by Jean Anouilh written in 1942. Besides being the only important play on the Antigone theme since Sophocles, this is a rare and remarkable instance of a modern presentation of an antique theme being at the same time an interpretation of it. It is therefore particularly meaningful in our attempt to uncover the germs in the Greek tragedies out of which the modern versions in their various forms have grown.

Anouilh's *Antigone* brings to light something in the *Antigone* of Sophocles which, as Reinhardt said, had remained enigmatic. As in the case of Hauptmann's *Iphigenia,* this is an archaic element which for good reason had been inaccessible to earlier interpreters. The relationship of Anouilh's *Antigone* to that of Sophocles, however, is quite different from the relationship between the Iphigenia plays of Hauptmann and Euripides. Hauptmann drew upon new, hitherto unknown material, new facts of archaic mythology. The case of Anouilh is much more complicated. Here we are not dealing with facts but with a sense of life—and an entirely modern one— which was able nevertheless to inspire a reinterpretation of Sophocles' *Antigone.* In this case the result is that the modern work illuminates the classical one and is illuminated by it to yield its own full meaning. This remarkable interaction (which of course emerges only from a fairly penetrating analysis of both works) is, to our knowledge, unique in the relationship between classical and modern Greek tragedies. Yet it entails no blurring of the differences and the lines of demarcation between the classical play and the modern one. On the contrary, this reciprocal clarification of meaning makes it possible to determine exactly where and in what sense Anouilh's *Antigone* represents a modernization of the *Antigone* of Sophocles.

There occurs in Anouilh a short sentence which seems to us to be the true key to the interpretation of this play and of Sophocles' *Antigone* as well, and to make comprehensible a whole series of passages in the latter that have always been difficult to interpret or have simply been passed over. After Antigone has been led away, Anouilh's Creon says : "Polynices was only a pretext."[7] But before going into Anouilh's play, let us see where this remark of Creon's leads if we follow it back into the Sophoclean play.

What about Sophocles' Polynices? It is notable that the events of the historical episode of the Seven against Thebes, in which Polynices and his brother Eteocles killed each other in single combat, are mentioned, but nothing is said about the brothers' character and conduct, except that the chorus refers to them as two unfortunate wretches, born of the same blood, who raised their spears against one another. Only the fact that Polynices may not be buried has a structural function in the play, specifically in relation to Antigone's action and character. This function is what makes it clear that Antigone is not inspired to her rebellious act of self-sacrifice by particularly strong personal, sisterly love. To Antigone's famous words to Creon—"It is my nature to join in love, not hate," which for so long were taken to express loving feminine gentleness —modern scholarship has restored the meaning they held for Greek antiquity : that her love is not personal, individual love but is exclusively love of family, of blood relatives (which is in fact how Hegel understood it). This interpretation finally makes contextual sense of a passage which Goethe could never reconcile with Antigone's words about joining in love and which he found so repellent that he told Eckermann that he wished it might be proved unauthentic.[8] This is the passage where Antigone says that she would never have assumed the burden of defying the king's decree for the sake of a child or a husband. She gives a very precise reason for this—one which appears very startling to modern sensibilities :

> What is the law that lies behind these words?
> One husband gone, I might have found another,
> or a child from a new man in first child's place,
> But with my parents hid away in death,
> no brother, ever, could spring up for me.[9]

This passage clearly states that her love and self-sacrifice apply only to the blood relationship. It is also symptomatic that no thought of Haemon, the man she is to marry, crosses her mind and that it is only from him that we learn of the betrothal at all. There is no scene between Antigone and Haemon alone.

With this in mind, we now perceive another relationship between Antigone's death and the action which leads to it, the burial of Polynices, a relationship which is almost the reverse of the one uppermost in our mental image of Antigone. "Polynices was only a pretext"—these words actually shed much light on the Sophoclean Antigone figure and indeed on the structure of the play itself. The crucial passage here occurs in the central speech of the scene between Antigone and Creon, where Antigone refers to the unwritten law of the underworld gods who require that a blood relation be buried.

> I knew I must die, even without your decree :
> I am only mortal. And if I must die
> Now, before it is my time to die,
> Surely this is no hardship: can anyone
> Living, as I live, with evil all about me,
> Think Death less than a friend? This death of mine
> Is of no importance; but if I had left my brother
> Lying in death unburied, I should have suffered.
> Now I do not.   (p. 203, Fitts and Fitzgerald translation)

The thing to notice here is the order in which the two motives are mentioned. "If I must die now, before it is my time to die, surely this is no hardship"—this expression of Antigone's readiness, one might even say her wish, to die precedes any mention of the action that will incur death. This might be taken to mean that she welcomes this action as the road that will lead her to Hades.

This passage alone of course would not suffice to confirm the hypothesis that behind Antigone's acknowledged motive for defying the king's decree, the obvious motive which precipitates the dramatic conflict, there is another one which, expressed as it is here, begins to look like the primary, more elemental one. There are, however, other passages which support the hypothesis. "You chose to live but I chose death," Antigone says to Ismene, when the latter offers to join her sister in her fate. A moment later she puts it even more strongly :

> Take heart. You live. My life died long ago.
> And that has made me fit to help the dead.
> (p. 178, Wyckoff translation)

This is the plainest passage. For here the connection of Antigone's death wish, her will to die, with her commitment to her blood relatives, to her "clan," is momentarily illuminated. The desire to die is in her because her relatives are dead, because "Persephone has called most of them home." Here we must refer again to the already quoted passage where Antigone says that she would not have defied the decree for anyone not related by blood, such as a husband or a child (which the mother does not feel to be a blood relative because, as she explains, she could conceive other children by other husbands).

But we must not jump to hasty conclusions. This relationship between Antigone's motives, in which the will for death is uppermost, is apparently suggested only in these few words, and we must ask whether they suffice to expose and explain the primacy of her death wish. Both the argument between Antigone and Creon and the one between Creon and Haemon hinge so absolutely on the question of justice that we are perhaps in danger of attributing a too crucial importance to what may be only casual words. But it is the outcome of the plot, the structure, and especially the ending of the play that show that Antigone's words are not casual or fortuitous; they lend these words a decisive weightiness and indeed shift the problem of *Antigone* to a more profound, more enigmatic level than the one of heroic action as such.

From this angle the Tiresias scene now takes on a new aspect. Tiresias appears after Antigone has been led away, and his appearance has always been related exclusively to Creon. Creon, caught in his own authoritarianism, is made aware of his injustice by Tiresias. The gods are angry with him because the dead man, who belongs to the gods of the underworld, is lying unburied and polluting the city and because Antigone, who belongs to the gods of the upper world, has been consigned to those of the netherworld. Only when calamity to his own house is prophesied does Creon capitulate and hurry to bury the dead Polynices and liberate Antigone. He comes too late; she has already hanged herself.

These elements in the action must not be disregarded. The fact that Antigone hangs herself before rescue arrives is a traditional fact of this epic legend. But a dramatist like Sophocles could not retain this element of chance simply as chance. Thus the "coming too late" has also been the subject of interpretation which, however, like the Tiresias scene itself, has invariably been related to Creon. Creon, says Reinhardt, is "the man who realizes too late. . . he comes too late, not because events move faster than might have been expected but because he is such a limited man" (p. 101). In a similar vein Walter Jens holds that Creon "still thinks that by merely rescinding his decree he can put a stop to what has long been determined. . . .But it is too late. In the end there is nothing but the lament of 'one who is now no more than nothing.' "[10] These explanations seem somehow unsatisfactory; in effect they read things into Creon's character and ignore the suicide motive as it applies to Antigone. Yet both the suicide and the "coming too late," as well as the whole Tiresias scene, acquire a more profound function, more firmly anchored in the structure of the tragedy, if they are seen in the light of Antigone's problem, that is, in the light of her will for death.

But we must read carefully and not disregard the factors which might contradict this view; we must pay particular attention to a major passage which indeed seems to do so—Antigone's lament, before she is led away, over having to depart from life before she has been a wife and mother :

> O tomb, vaulted bride-bed in eternal rock,
> Soon I shall be with my own again.
>
> (p. 221, Fitts and Fitzgerald translation)

> No marriage-bed, no marriage-song for me,
> and since no wedding, so no child to rear.
>
> (p. 190, Wyckoff translation)

Quite obviously these words contradict her earlier ones welcoming death. They contradict the idea that she is choosing death over life. Interpretation of apparently contradictory passages like these always runs the risk of explaining the contradictions psychologically and thus overlooking the work's mode of being, which is by no means that of irrational life, with its innumerable inherent contradictions. Thus when Reinhardt says that Antigone has "turned to face the realm of death" (p. 93) and is standing, before the end, on the borderline between the conflicting realms of the living and the dead (see note 12), this is a psychological and thus an essentially subjective explanation. According to Antigone's own words it is true, yet it explains nothing. We must discover why Sophocles puts into Antigone's mouth this affirmation of the will to live, which is to some extent a contradiction of her earlier words. If this question is to be satisfactorily answered, if, that is, it can be functionally fitted into the total structure of the play, the nature of the work reveals itself, stripped of everything accidental, and—by no means least important—the apparently fortuitous "coming too late" proves to be a poetic necessity and perfectly logical. Indeed, the construction of this play is so taut that this ending, this "coming too late," together with the related Tiresias scene, illuminates the earlier affirmation of the will to live and is illuminated by it; the one contributes to the understanding of the other.[11]

Let us take the Tiresias scene as our starting point. What does it mean if, instead of relating it *a priori* to Creon and his unmasking as a man, we relate it to Antigone? It denotes the possibility that she may be saved—a retarding element, or rather *the* retarding element, in the action. The vault is still not death. Creon says to the chorus :

> Take her, go!
> You know your orders: take her to the vault
> And leave her alone there. And if she lives or dies,
> That's her affair, not ours.
>
> (p. 221, Fitts and Fitzgerald translation)

The Tiresias scene ends with Creon rushing off to save Antigone. There is a good chance that she is still alive. So long as man lives, hope for rescue from a desperate situation lives too. And here the connection emerges between Antigone's affirmation of the will to live and the possibility of rescue. Those words are to be taken (or can be taken) as a counterpoint, as it were, to suicide before she can be rescued, as a link with the Tiresias scene, in which the possibility of rescue is implied, a possibility which might have shifted the balance of events in favor of life. The possibility of life is anticipated in Antigone's expression of the life wish. But the fact that rescue comes too late, which is contrary to what might be called the normal course of events, means in effect that Antigone's will for death is after all stronger than her will for life. The expression of her will to live fulfills the structural function of revealing the absolute primacy of her readiness for death. Creon and his fate do not matter; Reinhardt rightly recognizes that his fate is "empty." "He is left overwhelmed by misfortune rather than stricken at the very root of his being" (p. 102). But the emptiness of Creon's fate is not intended merely as a contrast to the meaningfulness of Antigone's, as Reinhardt believes. What Creon had been threatened with had to come to pass; as we have tried to show, the function of the threat is to introduce the possibility of rescue which, coming too late, in its turn shows up the primacy of Antigone's readiness for death.

The viewpoint of our comparative analysis seems to have been long forgotten, for up to now interpretation has been confined to the *Antigone* of Sophocles. In every point, however, it has followed the lead of the suggestive words spoken by Anouilh's Creon: "Polynices was only a pretext." Creon goes on : "For her the most important thing was to die." This is a key sentence in two senses. First, it unlocks the classical work; second, it indicates the line which separates the modern play from the Greek one. The line is marked by the modernization of the death problem itself. For now it is of the utmost importance not to let Anouilh's *Antigone* tempt us to interpret Sophocles' tragedy in a modern way. It is always tempting to do this when we can see a plausible death problem complex in a classical play. So we must carefully reexamine the Sophoclean Antigone's will for death and try to determine its nature.

It originates—objectively—in the firm rooting of her existence in the family, the clan. Now that the family of her blood relations is no more, her existence is deprived of the roots which sustain it.

> . . .with no friend's mourning,
> by what decree I go to the fresh-made prison-tomb.
> Alive to the place of corpses, an alien still,
> never at home with the living nor with the dead.
>
> (p. 188, Wyckoff translation)

Words like these draw even dying into the lostness of existence. Dying is hard because there are no loved ones to mourn. This lament finds its complement in the comforting assurance that she will be allowed to join her dead again :

> I come as a dear friend to my dear father,
> to you, my mother, and my brother too.
>
> (p. 189, Wyckoff translation)

The objective reason for Antigone's readiness for death, the reason of which she herself is aware, is that she has been forsaken by her blood relatives. But her sense of clan is so deeply involved with her sense of life—in a fact identical with it—that in this life situation her death wish and her clan feeling merge and lead to her dramatic action, in which they become one. In interpretation of this figure we can therefore say that she is a profoundly archaic one marked by a specifically chthonian sense of life. It is with good reason that she refers to the gods of the underworld, the chthonian gods whose commands she must obey.[12]

We emphasize this again because it is at this point that Antigone's modernization begins or becomes noticeable: the antique Antigone's archaic, chthonian sense of existence, nurturing an objective, conscious will for death, widens into a sense of existence less determinate and less conscious, of which death is a constituent part, to the point that the death feeling rises to existential dominance.

The reslanting of Sophocles' *Antigone* through this existential broadening of the sense of life is also expressed stylistically by the slightly parodistic form of Anouilh's play. Characters who speak and think in modern terms act out the old play again, with its ancient plot and all the details which are not applicable to its modern setting. "Well, here we are," says the prologue, stepping forward in the Shakespearean manner. "These people are about to act out for you the story of Antigone. Antigone is the thin little creature sitting over there. . . .She is going to have to play her part through to the end" (pp. 9–10). And later Creon says to Antigone : "I'm cast in the bad role, of course, and you in the good one" (p. 77). This has a double meaning, one in the context of the present action and a different one in that of its famous classical model which it must still follow, repeating and parodying it, if it is to be an Antigone play.

Let us look now at Creon's role. The rescue problem of the Tiresias scene in Sophocles is recognizable in an expanded form in the modern play, in which from the outset Creon himself represents the possibility of Antigone's being saved from death. In Anouilh Creon is a thoroughly humane man, a kind uncle who gave Antigone her first doll, as he reminds her. The parodistic split in his personality—already indicated in the prologue's description of him as a robustly built man with wrinkles who is tired and given to meditation—consists in his having issued the decree concerning Polynices and being obliged to enforce it on account of public opinion. At the same time he is a wise, skeptical realist, by no means greedy for power, who finds his own official duty and Antigone's resolution equally absurd. "I'm not going to let you die for a matter of politics," he tells her, and he makes every effort to bring her to her senses. He himself reveals to Antigone that her brothers were degenerate playboys, one worse than the other, not worth giving her life for—never mind sacrificing it to bury Polynices. In fact Anouilh's conception of Creon sheds considerable light on the Sophoclean tragedy, not so much on Creon's character as on his role and function, which the completely different character of the modern Creon now exposes. Something which in Sophocles emerges only in Creon's last-minute attempt to save Antigone is elaborated by Anouilh into a clearly recognizable function of his role as a potential rescuer (and there is now of course no further need for Tiresias). But in the face of the modern Antigone's will to die this function is as powerless as is Creon's last-minute attempt in Sophocles.

The relationship between the Antigone figures in Anouilh and Sophocles is analogous to that between their Creons. The decisive point, as we have said, is the death problem underlying both characterizations, though in different forms. Seen this way, all the details of the modern play fit together, just as those of the classical tragedy combine in a unified structure.

Let us begin with the least accentuated element in Sophocles : Antigone's will to live, expressed toward the end in the lament that she will never be a wife or mother, and finally overcome by her will to die. This lament brings out the striking fact that Haemon, her future husband, has no part in her thoughts and that there is no scene between the two of them alone. This is indeed striking, but, as we believe we can show, for this very reason it confirms that Antigone's will to live is weaker than her will to die. In Anouilh her will to live is depicted more colorfully yet more vaguely, as though the girl herself did not quite understand it. Here Haemon plays a role in Antigone's feelings too. She loves this man, who has suddenly turned away from the beautiful, serene, worldly Ismene in favor of plain, scrawny, not to say ugly Antigone. She says she would have been proud to be his wife and even wanted to give herself to him before she died. She is under a compulsion; she is not wholly in control of her own being and willing. She admits to Creon that it is absurd to die for an unburied corpse, and when he asks her for whose sake, then, she is really making this gesture, she can find no answer but : "For nobody. For myself." This is the decisive admission; it is repeated again and confirmed in the farewell letter to Haemon that she dictates to the guard : "I don't even know any more what I'm dying for" (p. 119). This is the statement of the unconscious existential will for death which Creon's words "Polynices was only a pretext" confirm and by which they are confirmed. The very words of Sophocles' Antigone to Ismene—"You chose to live but I chose death"—are repeated in Anouilh, and this in itself shows exactly how and where the two works are linked. The sense of clan has become irrelevant to the modern mind; it is completely eliminated through Creon's exposure of Polynices and Eteocles, and it is this that brings into the open the existential contingency of Antigone's death will.

Nevertheless there is an element in the sense of life of Anouilh's Antigone which corresponds to the conscious, objective ground for the Greek Antigone's will for death and which even points up the modern Antigone's absoluteness of character. This element stands in the same ambivalent relationship to her will for death as the clan feeling does in the Greek Antigone, so that it is not quite clear which is cause and which is effect. Antigone says an unconditional *no* where her uncle, making concessions to life's eventualities, says a conditional *yes*. The discussion of *yes* and *no,* which is the core of their argument, contains the whole problem complex and dialectic of man's freedom and non-freedom. Creon says with some justification that it is easier to say *no* than to say *yes*. "It is easy to say *no*. . . .To say *yes* you have to sweat and roll up your sleeves, take hold of life with both hands and get into it up to the elbows. It is easy to say *no,* even if it means dying. All you have to do is sit still and wait" (p. 86).

But this is the sensitive, problematical point. The *no* entails freedom from any duty in life, but it equally entails an absoluteness which, if followed through to the point of sacrificing life, annuls this freedom. Antigone wants everything or nothing—she would not even want or love Haemon any longer (although she is in love with him) if she did not possess him totally and absolutely, if he "stops growing pale with fear when I grow pale, stops thinking I'm dead when I am five minutes late, stops feeling that he is alone in the world and hating me when I laugh and he doesn't know why"

(p. 98). She is the daughter of Oedipus and "she asks [her] questions to the bitter end," long after the tiny chance of hope has vanished —"your dear, dirty hope!" (p. 100)—the hope, say, that she may still be saved. This is one of the grounds, one of the reasons, that make life not worth living to the modern Antigone; it corresponds to what makes it seem worthless to the Greek one. But it only corresponds to it; it is not the same thing; it differs from it in propor tion to the less clearly defined sense of life that differentiates the modern mode of experiencing and its literary embodiment from the classical one. The sense of life of Sophocles' Antigone is oriented toward death because her relatives are dead, that of Anouilh's Antigone is oriented toward death because life itself does not meet the absoluteness of her demands, so that she rejects it as contemptible, as Sophocles' Antigone rejects hers. But when she says at the end that she no longer even knows what she is dying for, this suggests a general attitude to life in which it is a simple fact that life may be dominant for one person, as it is for Ismene, and death for another, one case being just as irrational as the other. As the unidentified chorus finally puts it, when all those who had to die have died, it makes no difference what this man or that man believed, whether they understood any of it or not. If it had not been for little Antigone, they would all have had their peace. But her death too will be forgotten by those still alive; they will go on waiting for their own death, like Creon, or playing cards, like the guards.

These closing words of the modern French play are certainly a far cry from their Greek model, Sophocles. But the distance does not represent an absolute antithesis so much as a reshaping—an extreme one, to be sure—of an enigmatic element in the classical work in such a way that this modern reshaping brings it into focus. Such is the special interpretive function of Anouilh's *Antigone,* which for its own part is the Antigone of an age accustomed to thinking existentially. Being toward death is one of the fundamental existential principles in Heidegger's *Sein und Zeit.*

This concept and Anouilh's Antigone problem in particular bring up the name of Kierkegaard. Here again we venture to draw upon a theoretical and philosophical interpretation (as we did with Bloch's interpretation of Helen)—this time in order to confirm the value of Anouilh's modern Antigone for the interpretation of her classical counterpart.

Kierkegaard too developed the classical Antigone into a modern figure, and his interpretation and transformation of her is not altogether foreign to Anouilh's. Despite the differences between them, Kierkegaard's interpretation is in fact related to Anouilh's since it too centers on a tragic sense of life and not only on a tragic situation, as in Hegel. In the chapter entitled "The Ancient Tragic Motif as Reflected in the Modern" in *Entweder-Oder (Either/Or)*, he contrasts Sophocles' Antigone with a "modern" one, whom he calls "our Antigone, the bride of sorrow."[13] For Kierkegaard, however, this sorrow "rests like an impenetrable sorrow over the whole family" (p. 153); it has pervaded its life since Antigone's father incurred his unhappy fate and tragic guilt. He holds that to take Antigone's defiance of the king's decree "as a isolated fact, as a collision between sisterly affection and piety and an arbitrary human prohibition" (p. 154) is to misunderstand the nature of the Greek tragedy. Precisely this, which most interpreters, following Hegel's lead, have taken to be the tragic situation of Sophocles' Antigone, Kierkegaard calls a modern tragic theme. By contrast "that which in the Greek sense affords the tragic interest is that Oedipus' sorrowful destiny re-echoes in the brother's unhappy death, in the sister's collision with a simple human prohibition; it is, so to say, the after affects, the tragic destiny of Oedipus, ramifying in every branch of his family. This is the totality which makes the sorrow of the spectator so infinitely deep" (p. 154).

Kierkegaard does not quote any passages in support of this. But his whole case could be derived from Antigone's first words to Ismene :

> You would think that we had already suffered enough
> For the curse on Oedipus.
>
> > (p. 185, Fitts and Fitzgerald translation)

This passage, however, contradicts the further conclusion—and this is perhaps why Kierkegaard did not quote it—which distinguishes his imaginary modern Antigone from the Greek one. The antique Antigone, he says, "is not at all concerned about her father's unhappy destiny. . . .Antigone lives as carefree as any other young Grecian maiden. . .[so that] if it were not for the disclosure of this new fact [the burial of her brother] we might imagine her life as very happy in its gradual unfolding" (pp. 153–154). This then is the point where the Greek outlook can be transformed into a modern one in an Antigone who is "not turned outward but inward," that is to say, who is conscious in her inmost being of the sorrow, the hereditary sorrow, of the race and is formed by it. "Her real life is concealed. . .[and therefore] although she is living, she is in another sense dead" (p. 155). The bride of sorrow, "she dedicates her life to sorrow over her father's destiny, over her own" (p. 156).

Kierkegaard now gives a description of this imaginary Antigone, always mindful of her sorrow, which sounds like an analysis of an existing work. It is indeed a conception similar to Anouilh's modern Antigone, who is conscious of her death wish but not—or only vaguely—of its origin. In Kierkegaard's Antigone too there exists in this knowledge "an ignorance which can always keep sorrow in movement, always transform it into pain" (p. 159), but Kierkegaard explains this element of ignorance more precisely than Anouilh does. It applies to Antigone's uncertainty as to whether her father was aware of his guilt, a guilt which she believes she shares as his loving daughter and as a member of the family. Kierkegaard finds a modern motivating factor in this which does not exist in the antique Antigone, for whom "her father's guilt and suffering is an external fact, an immovable fact, which her sorrow does not alter" (p. 158), that is, it does not stimulate reflection, which is needed to make sorrow a completely inward "substantial" state—for this is how these associations are to be understood. This notion of the "substantial" probably approximates closely the notion of the "existential." We need not concern ourselves here with Kierkegaard's analysis of Antigone's sorrow, which on this particular point is somewhat abstruse. What is important for us is the fact that his modern Antigone is conceived in an existential instead of merely an ethical manner. Moreover, for him the classical Antigone already contains the germ of this conception. All the requisite elements for depicting her as "modern," as the bride of "substantial" sorrow, are present in her. Characteristically, she is said, in the passage already quoted, to be already dead, although still living. But the germ from which this interpretation springs shows itself to be closely related to an essential factor concealed in Sophocles' Antigone which, as we believe we have shown, accounts for her death wish :

namely, her commitment to the family, to the clan. For Kierkegaard this bond is the source of the sorrow of family guilt, of
Antigone's existence as a bride of sorrow, which already points to
that leaning toward death which becomes her dominant sense of
existence.

But this is just what separates the existential viewpoint of our
own time from Kierkegaard's : Anouilh offers no specific factual
explanation corresponding to Kierkegaard's attribution of Antigone's
sorrow to her ignorance of Oedipus' relation to his guilt. Kierkegaard's "modern Antigone" is useful to the topic of this chapter if
only because it shows in principle the possibility of existential interpretations of the Greek Antigone and thus helps to clarify Anouilh's
play in its interpretive function and its significance for the Antigone
problem.[14]

Clearly these deeply existential versions of the Antigone theme
do not exhaust the subject. It would indeed be curious if dramatists
in a time like ours, who have experienced the problems of might
and right in the stark reality of war and dictatorship, had missed
the obvious aspect of the Antigone figure, her courageous personality. Antigone, whom Brecht called "the great figure of resistance,"
stands very much in the foreground of literary consciousness and it
is easy to understand why both the first and the second world wars
called attention to her. In 1947 Brecht adapted Hölderlin's translation of the *Antigone*;[15] in 1917 Walter Hasenclever created a
"figure of resistance" who without doubt possesses far more immediacy than Brecht's.

The latter point is not mentioned merely as a fact but as the
point of departure for an assessment of the two versions. Exactly
thirty years separate Hasenclever's work from Brecht's, and the
times when the two plays were written are significant. Although
Brecht called Sophocles' Antigone the great figure of resistance in
classical tragedy, he added that in the year 1947 "her poem could
not be written here."[16] For the term "resistance," familiar to all
those who lived through the Nazi era, had nothing in common with
Antigone's resistance. "She does not represent the German resistance
fighters who must seem most important to us," says Brecht. He
thinks that "the ancient play, being so distant in time, did not invite
identification with its heroine" (p. 100). But historical distance is

perhaps not so essential as the type of resistance which Antigone represents. Pursuing Brecht's ideas, we might say that a personal confrontation with a tyrant, like Antigone's relatively straightforward action in defying Creon's prohibition, was a gesture of resistance unthinkable under totalitarian dictatorship, where resistance consisted in the attempt to eliminate that dictatorship and in working clandestinely to that end. One might even say that the human, personal factor, which, despite all Creon's tyranny, still persists in his relationship with Antigone and in their discussion, is the very factor which in the year 1947 made any identification with Antigone impossible. Brecht evidently gave his adaptation the title *The Antigone of Sophocles* to prevent its being taken as something possible in our time. Consequently he does not seek to make his Antigone play "worth seeing" as a demonstration of Antigone's problem but as an exemplification of "the role of the use of force in the collapse of top government," which is a far more abstract phenomenon.

These remarks of Brecht's in the preface to his Antigone play are almost more instructive than his treatment of the play itself, which formally might be called a composition (using Hölderlinian language), largely translated into the Brecht idiom and built around Hölderlinian thematic key words—a complex affair since Hölderlin's text is itself a translation. Behind the verbal lattice work of this Hölderlinian-Brechtian text the actual figure of Antigone emerges with little change; all its essential elements have been retained and are underlined in every case by the original words of Hölderlin's text. In some passages resistance to Creon's decree is already expressed as resistance to or a critique of the rule of dictatorship :

> Where you need force against others
> you soon need it against your own. (p. 44)

But the major change Brecht makes, in line with the intention stated in his preface, is that Antigone's problem is superseded by the more universal one of tyranny perishing in and of itself. For this purpose he introduces a situation of political warfare precipitated by Creon to divert attention from the domestic consequences of his rule—and here the topical allusion is obvious. The role of Tiresias as a prophet is limited to seeing through these events and their motives and foretelling the inevitability of ruin :

What foolishness or evil have you done
that you must go on committing foolishness and evil? . . .
Robbery comes from robbery and hardness needs hardness
and more needs more and in the end is nothing.   (p. 80)

In a sense Brecht carries *ad absurdum* Hegel's old interpretation : that Creon also represents a rightful duty. And the objection
to Hegel's view which already arises out of the Sophoclean plot—
that Creon would have to stand by his decree even when the seer
foretells disastrous consequences for him—is worked up into a
capital theme by Brecht. For his Creon acts on purely utilitarian
grounds; it is no longer fear of the gods' retribution that drives him
to the vault to rescue Antigone but the necessity of securing
Haemon's services as leader of his army, since he has been informed
that his eldest son Megareus has been killed in battle.

The thirty years that separate the two German Antigones of
Hasenclever and Brecht are, as we have said, symptomatic of their
understanding of this great figure of resistance. For Brecht there
was no connection between Antigone's resistance and the resistance
movement of the 1940's, which fought not to defend human right
against state right but to abolish a criminal dictatorship and to
restore a nation's freedom and honor. Antigone's personal problem
had to yield to the problem of power and its fate. In 1917 there
was no analogous situation in any of the warring European coun-
tries. Resistance was not yet a reality but at best an idea, a genuine
revolutionary idea (realized in Russia that same year) born of war
weariness and directed against the form of government responsible
for that war. In Hasenclever's *Antigone,* freely created on the
Sophoclean model, the war plays this very role, its pros and cons
argued out between "voices" loyal to the monarchy and revolutionary ones.
    In Germany, however, World War I was also the era of literary
Expressionism, and as an Expressionist dramatist Hasenclever was
able to find in Sophocles, either in full view or immediately beneath
the surface, everything which the Expressionists were hurling against
society and their own time : resistance to the power of the state,
resistance to the war, the proclamation of humanity and fraternity,
love and life. Antigone's most famous line—"It is my nature to join
in love, not hate"—can be taken as the key to Hasenclever's

Antigone, as its revolutionary theme, though it is never cited in this sense. His Antigone becomes a revolutionary, rising above the personal deed of sisterly love to proclaim before the people the message of love for humanity. At first the people, still loyal to the monarchy, threaten her, only to kneel before her when she declares :

> I gave my brother back to the earth
> and celebrate with you resurrection.
> Now we are brothers in pain!
> Now I know: women can be immortal,
> when they water men's meaningless ways
> from the pitcher of love;
> when from tears of their poverty
> help sprouts;
> when the act of the living heart
> razes enmity's walls.[17]

But even if it might look as though Antigone's death sacrifice for the sake of bringing love into this world is going to initiate a better, more humane era—the hope she expresses herself in the vault : "I have helped. My work is done"—this hope is extinguished again. When the people find themselves free after Creon's breakdown and departure, they want to storm and plunder the castle. Yet there is no doubt that this Antigone's doctrine of love and her self-sacrificial death point to the teaching and sacrificial death of Jesus, indeed to the Messianic hope of his second coming :

> Fellow men! In a thousand years
> I shall be walking among you.

But even though Hasenclever brings the light of the mystery of Christ to bear on his Antigone, it does nothing to illuminate the riddle of the great archetypal figure, who stands in the vast arena of world literature and the human consciousness looking more monumental than ever against an interpretation of this kind. And this is how she looks in the light of Anouilh's modern version, precisely because it has come closer to her secret than any other.

EPILOGUE

Having reached the end of our brief excursion through a thousand years of literary history, let us refer back to the introduction and restate the method and nature of our presentation. The presentation should by now have made it clear that it was never intended as an exhaustive, chronological, historical study of thematic elements in the strict sense. What we were trying to do was set up and treat the subject of the classical and modern renderings of the Greek tragic heroes and heroines in such a way that in practically every case one single modern work provided the starting point for the analysis and defined the problem (even when that work was not the first one we dealt with). These works were: Sartre's *The Flies,* Giraudoux's *Electra,* Hauptmann's *Iphigenia,* Wilder's *Alcestiad,* Braun's *Medea,* and Anouilh's *Antigone.* This procedure was effective, we believe, because these are the key modern works on their respective subjects. For the same reason these works also showed that the germs of their thematic problems were present, though usually hidden, in the classical models and showed too how these problems unfolded. Thus the changes in the antique tragic figures are a graphic index to the human mind's conception of itself in any particular age. New changes in man's image will doubtless produce new reshapings of these Greek models, which mark the beginning of Western intellectual history. For, as Gottfried Benn wrote, "Millennia are living in our minds. . . .The Atridae flourish the thyrsus."

NOTES

Quotations from the Greek tragedies, unless otherwise noted, taken from *The Complete Greek Tragedies,* ed. David Grene and Richard Lattimore (Chicago: University of Chicago Press, 1953–59). References are to individual volumes in this series.

Except where otherwise noted, quotations from the modern French and German works have been translated from the originals by the present translator.

INTRODUCTION

1. Corneille, *Discours sur le poème dramatique,* in *Oeuvres* (Paris, 1862), I, 56.
2. Hegel, *Vorlesungen über die Ästhetik,* 2nd ed., ed. Hotho (Berlin, 1843), III, 362.
3. *Andromache* in *Euripides,* III, trans. John Frederick Nims, p. 70.
4. See Walter Jens's essay "Antikes und modernes Drama" in *Jahresring* 1960–61, p. 81.
5. For a treatment of this kind, see K. Heinemann, *Die tragischen Gestalten der Griechen in der Weltliteratur* (Leipzig, 1920). Also E. Frenzel, *Stoffe der Weltliteratur* (Stuttgart, 1962).
6. For this reason no analysis of other interpretations has been attempted, but selective references are given to the relevant literature.

1   CLYTEMNESTRA

1. Aeschylus, *Agamemnon,* in *Ten Greek Plays,* ed. L. R. Lind, trans. Louis MacNeice (Boston: Houghton Mifflin, 1957), p. 51.

169

2. See M. P. Nilsson, *Griechischer Glaube* (Bern, 1950), pp. 65 ff.
3. *Agamemnon,* p. 72.

2   ORESTES

1. Ulrich von Wilamowitz-Moellendorff, *Griechische Tragödien* (Berlin, 1919), II, 128.
2. *The Libation Bearers,* in *Aeschylus,* I, trans. Lattimore, p. 103.
3. W. F. Otto, *Theophania* (Hamburg: Rowohlt, 1956), pp. 99, 102.
4. Martin Heidegger, *Sein und Zeit* (Halle, 1927), p. 282.
5. *The Eumenides,* in *Aeschylus,* I, trans. Lattimore, p. 142.
6. *Electra,* in *Euripides,* V, trans. Emily Townsend Vermeule, p. 59.
7. *Orestes,* in *Euripides,* IV, trans. William Arrowsmith, p. 130.
8. In connection with this truly striking change in Orestes' psychological situation, M. Pohlenz recalls the popular Greek philosophical idea that man can overcome even the most violent emotions if external events or his own will divert him to other things. *Die griechische Tragödie,* 2nd ed. (Göttingen, 1954), p. 418.
9. *Iphigenia in Tauris,* in *Euripides,* II, trans. Witter Bynner, p. 145.
10. *Orestes,* p. 206.
11. Jean-Paul Sartre, *Les mouches* (Paris: Gallimard, 1947), p. 83.
12. Sartre, *L'existentialisme est un humanisme* (Paris, 1946), pp. 36–37.
13. *Ibid.,* p. 25.
14. Oskar Seidlin, "The Oresteia Today: A Myth Dehumanized," in his *Essays in German and Comparative Literature* (Chapel Hill: University of North Carolina Press, 1961), p. 249.
15. T. S. Eliot, *The Family Reunion* (New York: Harcourt Brace, 1939).

3   ELECTRA

1. *Electra,* in *Sophocles,* II, trans. Grene, p. 164.
2. Hugo von Hofmannsthal, *Elektra,* in *Gesammelte Werke,* Dramen, II (Frankfurt, 1954), p. 50.
3. Jean Giraudoux, *Electre,* in *Théâtre,* III (Paris: Grasset, 1959), p. 16.
4. Giraudoux, *Elektra,* trans. Hans Rothe (Munich: List), p. 138.
5. Hofmannsthal, *Aufzeichnungen* (Frankfurt, 1959), p. 217.
6. Jens also identifies this problem with the guilt and fate of Hofmannsthal's Electra. *Hofmannsthal und die Griechen* (Tübingen, 1955), p. 66, footnote.
7. Cf. Wolfgang Schadewaldt, "Sophocles und das Leid," in *Hellas und Hesperien* (Zurich and Stuttgart, 1960), especially pp. 241 ff.

8. Sigmund Freud, *General Introduction to Psychoanalysis,* trans. Joan Riviere (New York: Liveright, 1920), especially pp. 184 and 290 ff.
9. Freud, *An Outline of Psychoanalysis,* trans. James Strachey (New York: Norton, 1949), p. 95.
10. Eugene O'Neill, *Mourning Becomes Electra* (New York: Liveright, 1931), p. 53.
11. Schadewaldt, "Daten zur *Elektra* des Sophokles," in *Hellas und Hesperien,* p. 296.

4 IPHIGENIA

1. *Iphigenia in Aulis,* in *Euripides,* IV, trans. C. R. Walker, p. 279.
2. Noted by C. F. W. Behl in *Zwiesprache mit Gerhart Hauptmann* (Munich, 1948), p. 49.
3. Schiller, "Anmerkungen zu *Iphingenie in Aulis,*" *Säkular-Ausgabe,* XVI, p. 104.
4. Ernst Howald, *Die griechische Tragödie* (Zurich, 1930), p. 161.
5. *Iphigenia in Tauris,* in *Euripides,* II, trans. Witter Bynner, p. 124.
6. Goethe, *Iphigenie auf Tauris,* lines 1712–1717.
7. See Hans Jensen, *Die Sage von der Iphigenie in Delphi in der deutschen Dichtung* (Münster, 1911).
8. Goethe became interested in this subject while he was in Italy, working on his *Iphigenie.* In the *Italienische Reise* entry for October 19, 1786, he outlines the content and "argument" of an "Iphigenie auf Delphos."
9. The *Fabulae* of Hyginus narrate the stories of the Greek tragedies, including many that have not survived. He took the legend of Iphigenia in Delphi from a lost play of Sophocles.
10. See Pauly-Wissowa, *Realencyclopädie der klassischen Alterumswissenschaft,* IX, supplement, 1916.
11. Gerhart Hauptmann, *Die Atridentetralogie* (Berlin, 1949).
12. Pauly-Wissowa, *op. cit.,* p. 2593.
13. See my essay "Das Opfer der delphischen Iphigenie," in *Wirkendes Wort,* 1953–54, IV. Also Seidlin's comparison (in *Essays*) of Hauptmann's Hecatean Iphigenia with Goethe's humanistic one, to the distinct detriment of the former.
14. Behl notes only one brief remark by Hauptmann on this subject, dated September 14, 1940: "Now I really must write an Iphigenia in Aulis. . . .I cannot get rid of an inner compulsion to show what led up to Iphigenia's final act of sacrifice" (*Zwiesprache,* p. 48).

5   HELEN

1. *The Trojan Women,* in *Euripides,* III, trans. Lattimore, p. 132.
2. Giraudoux, *La guerre de Troie n'aura pas lieu,* in *Théâtre,* II, 380.
3. Goethe, *Faust,* Part II, lines 9254-44, trans. Charles E. Passage (Indianapolis: Bobbs-Merrill, 1965).
4. Ernst Bloch, *Das Prinzip Hoffnung* (Frankfurt, 1959), I, 210.
5. The "wisp of fiery air" interpreted by Bloch as "the luminous vestige of the dream" which the Trojan Helen has lived for ten years is evidently Bloch's own reshaping of the Euripidean text, where the messenger reports merely that Helen has "risen invisibly to Heaven."
6. Hofmannsthal, "Die ägyptische Helena," in *Werke,* Prosa, IV, 443.
7. *Odyssey,* Book IV, lines 259–264, trans. Robert Fitzgerald (New York: Doubleday, 1963).
8. Hofmannsthal, *Die ägyptische Helena,* in *Werke,* Dramen, IV, 240.
9. Wolfgang Hildesheimer's version of Helen in his delightfully sophisticated radio play *Das Opfer Helena,* published in *Sprich, damit ich dich höre* (Munich, List, 1961), is based on a different sober "truth." This is another rehabilitation of Helen, as surprising as it is cold-bloodedly realistic; here she is presented as a victim of Spartan and Trojan politics. Both Menelaus and Paris, the latter passively, the former actively, want to arrange Helen's abduction as a welcome pretext for war and conquest. Helen herself, however irresponsible, is thus vindicated as the only person in her whole environment having pure motives and feelings.

6   ALCESTIS

1. Thornton Wilder, *The Alcestiad.* Translator's note: This play has never been published in English. The quotations from it in this chapter have been translated from the German text, *Die Alkestiade,* trans. Herbert E. Herlitschka (Frankfurt and Hamburg: Fischer, 1960).
2. See Wilamowitz, III, 69.
3. An *Alcestis* by Phrynicus was already in existence. It emphasized the burlesque elements, such as the drunken Fates and the figure of Hercules.
4. *Alcestis,* in *Euripides,* I, trans. Lattimore, p. 8.
5. Hofmannsthal, *Alkestis,* in *Werke,* Dramen, I, 18.
6. Wieland, *Alceste,* in *Gesammelte Schriften,* Part I, Vol. IX (Berlin, 1931).
7. Since we have mentioned Goethe in connection with Wieland's *Alceste,* it should not be overlooked that nobody made more fun of

this work than he did in his satire *Götter, Helden und Wieland,* written, to be sure, in 1773, a decade before his own humanization of Euripides, his "devilishly humane" Iphigenia.

8. From the numerous eighteen-century versions of the Alcestis story we selected Wieland's as being the best-known example to illuminate the Admetus problem. Other Alcestis plays and operas of this period show that Admetus' acceptance of the sacrifice was found offensive, and Alcestis is therefore made to act without his knowledge. See Heinemann, *Die tragischen Gestalten, op. cit.;* G. Ellinger, *Alkestis in der modernen Literatur* (Halle, 1888); K. Steinwender, *Alkestis— vom Altertum bis zur Gegenwart* (dissertation, Vienna, 1951); and K. von Fritz, "Euripides' *Alkestis* und ihre modernen Nachahmer und Kritiker," in *Antike und moderne Tragödie* (Berlin, 1962).

    Particular mention should be made of J. G. Herder's little "drama with songs," *Admetos' Haus* (1803) because of a motif which reappears in E. W. Eschmann's modern version (discussed on p. 115), where the gods themselves restore Alcestis to life not merely because of her sacrifice but also in response to Admetus' love.

9. Rainer Maria Rilke, *Requiem and Other Poems,* trans. J. B. Leishman (London: Hogarth Press, 1949), p. 102.

10. In his essay "Rilke und die Antike" in *Antike und Abendland* (1948), III, 207, Ernst Zinn shows that here Rilke was following Wilamowitz's assertion that in the lost versions of the Alcestis story the events all took place at the wedding.

11. Alexander Lernet-Holenia, *Alkestis,* in *Die Trophäe,* II (Zurich, 1946).

12. For example, the words in which Admetus begs the god to grant him a reprieve (p. 54) and the stage direction: "Alcestis comes down a street of guests." She then speaks to the god, as she does in Rilke.

13. Mention should be made of R. Prechtl's *Alkestis* (1917), discussed by both Heinemann and Steinwender, which deals with the struggle between the will to live and the fear of death, and thus strengthens a motif which also appears in Lernet-Holenia and Eschmann as part of the death problem.

7   PHAEDRA

1. *Hippolytus,* in *Euripides,* I, trans. Grene, p. 163.

2. In Seneca's *Phaedra,* from which Racine borrowed a number of plot elements, Phaedra also confesses before her death.

3. Robinson Jeffers, *The Cretan Woman,* in *Hungerfield and Other Poems* (New York: Random House, 1951), pp. 42–43.

4. The same is true of D'Annunzio's *Fedra* (1909). This work, beautiful as its verse is, requires no more than passing mention because it contributes nothing new or interesting to the Phaedra problem, despite considerable expansion of the action, as for instance through the episode of the Theban slave sent to Hippolytus and murdered by Phaedra in her passionate jealousy. Yet it is not true, as Heinemann asserts, that Phaedra's love "wallows in a mire of sensuality." The distinctive feature, if any, of this Phaedra play is its depiction of an absolute erotic passion, especially at the end when, over the dead body of Hippolytus and before the bow of Artemis, the new moon, Phaedra acknowledges to Theseus his son's innocence and her own treachery. Before dying she declares her devotion to the man who has spurned her in the words: "Ippolito, son' teco" ("Hippolytus, I am yours").

8 MEDEA

1. Jean Anouilh, *Médée* (Paris: La Table Ronde, 1953), p. 38.
2. Wilamowitz, III, 170 ff. See also Karl Kerenyi, *Töchter der Sonne* (Zurich, 1944) on the tradition of this legend.
3. *Medea,* in *Euripides,* I, trans. Rex Warner, p. 77.
4. Grillparzer, *Medea,* Act III.
5. Matthias Braun, *Die Troerinnen und Medea* (Frankfurt: Fischer, 1959).
6. Robinson Jeffers' *Medea* (1946) is a modern version only insofar as language and style go. It also retains the Aegeus scene.
7. Hans Henny Jahnn, *Medea* (Frankfurt: Europäische Verlagsanstalt, 1959).

9 OEDIPUS

1. See Peter Szondi, *Versuch über das Tragische* (Wiesbaden, 1961), pp. 65 ff., in which the tragic happening is entirely explained by the effects and interaction of the three prophecies.
2. See B. M. W. Knox's subtle analysis of the connection between the character of Oedipus and the process of disclosure in *Oedipus at Thebes* (New Haven: Yale University Press, 1957), pp. 29 ff.
3. André Gide, *Oedipe,* in *Théâtre* (Paris: Gallimard, 1947).
4. Hofmannsthal, *Ödipus und die Sphinx,* in *Werke, Dramen,* II, 294.

10 ANTIGONE

1. Karl Reinhardt, *Sophokles,* 3rd ed. (Frankfurt, 1948), pp. 88 ff.

2. *Antigone,* in *The Oedipus Cycle,* trans. Dudley Fitts and Robert Fitzgerald (New York: Harcourt, Brace & World, 1966), p. 203.

3. Hegel, *Vorlesungen über die Ästhetik,* III, 556.

4. Hegel, *Vorlesungen über die Philosophie der Religion* (Leipzig, 1927), II, 156.

5. See H. Weinstock, *Sophles* (Leipzig, 1931), pp. 96–126.

6. Schadewaldt, *Hellas und Hesperien,* pp. 276 ff.

7. Anouilh, *Antigone* (Paris: La Table Ronde, 1944), p. 105.

8. Goethe, *Conversations with Eckermann,* March 28, 1827.

9. *Antigone,* in *Sophocles,* I, trans. Elizabeth Wyckoff, p. 190.

10. Jens, "Antigone Interpretationen" in *Satura* (Baden-Baden, 1952), p. 58.

11. It should be noted that Sophocles' *Antigone* can also be analyzed on the assumption that it *does* contain contradictions. Tycho von Wilamowitz-Moellendorff's "Die dramatische Technik des Sophokles," in *Philologische Untersuchungen,* XXII (Berlin, 1917), a work much quoted by Sophocles scholars, even tries to show that Sophocles was concerned only with what contributed to the immediate stage effect and ignored motivational insufficiencies or contradictions.

12. Not until this book was in press did I come across a little known lecture of Karl Kerenyi entitled *Dionysos und das Tragische in der Antigone* (Frankfurt, 1935), which brings out Antigone's turning toward the realm of Hades. Kerenyi calls this "her being Persephone" (p. 13). He even compares it to "the purely chthonian being of flowers, which are most perfectly dedicated to non-being" (p. 12). This view, which, as we have mentioned in the text, is also evident in Reinhardt, provides welcome support for our interpretation derived from the structure of the play and from perspectives opened up by Anouilh.

13. Soren Kierkegaard, *Either/Or,* trans. David F. Swenson (New York: Doubleday, 1959), I, 156.

14. For a deeper understanding of this and of Antigone's place in Kierkegaard's system of ideas, see Rehm's discussion of Kierkegaard's Antigone in *Begegnungen und Probleme* (Bern, 1957).

15. Bertolt Brecht, *Die Antigone des Sophokles,* in *Stücke,* XI (Frankfurt, 1959).

16. Brecht, *Vorwort zu "Antigonemodell 1948",* ibid., p. 99.

17. Walter Hasenclever, *Antigone* (Berlin, 1918), pp. 56–57.

LIST OF PLAYS
DISCUSSED

Vittorio Alfieri
  Agamemnon

Aeschylus
  The Oresteia:
  Agamemnon
  The Libation Bearers
  The Eumenides

Jean Anouilh
  Médée
  Antigone

Matthias Braun
  Medea

Bertolt Brecht
  Die Antigone des Sophokles

Pierre Corneille
Oedipe

Gabriele D'Annunzio
Fedra

T. S. Eliot
The Family Reunion

Ernst Wilhelm Eschmann
Alkestis

Euripides
Electra
Orestes
The Trojan Women
Helen
Alcestis
Hippolytus (Phaedra)
Medea
Iphigenia in Tauris
Iphigenia in Aulis

André Gide
Oedipe

Jean Giraudoux
Electre
La guerre de Troie n'aura pas lieu (*Tiger at the Gates*)

Wolfgang von Goethe
Iphigenie auf Tauris

Franz Grillparzer
Medea

Walter Hassenclever
Antigone

Gerhart Hauptmann
Die Atridentetralogie:
Iphigenie in Delphi
Iphigenie in Aulis
Agamemnons Tod and *Elektra*

Johann Gottfried von Herder
Admetos Haus

Wolfgang Hildesheimer
Das Opfer Helena

Hugo von Hofmannsthal
Elektra
Die ägyptische Helena
Alkestis
Ödipus und die Sphinx

Hans Henny Jahnn
Medea

Robinson Jeffers
The Cretan Woman
Medea

Alexander Lernet-Holenia
Alkestis

Eugene O'Neill
Mourning Becomes Electra

R. Prechtl
Alkestis

Jean Racine
Phèdre

Rainer Maria Rilke
"Alcestis"

Jean Paul Sartre
Les mouches (The Flies)

Sophocles
Electra
Oedipus Rex
Antigone

Voltaire
Oedipe

Christoph Martin Wieland
Alceste

Thornton Wilder
The Alcestiad

INDEX

Achilles, 7, 9

Admetus: legend of, 102–3; in Euripides, 103–5; in Hofmannsthal, 105–7; in Lernet-Holenia, 114; in Rilke, 113; in Wieland, 107–8, 173n; in Wilder, 109

Admetos Haus (Herder), 173n

Aegeus, 131–2

Aegisthus, 37–8, 63

Aeschylus: on Cassandra, 18–20; on Clytemnestra, 17–20; on Electra, 46–7; and free will, 20; *The Eumenides*, 23, 27–9; *The Libation Bearers*, 22–3; 25–6; *Oresteia*, 17–20

Agamemnon, 15–6, 71–2, 86–7

Agamemnon (Alfieri), 16–7, 21

Agamemnon's Death (Hauptmann), 21, 78, 88

Agamemnons Tod (Hauptmann), 21, 78, 88

Ägyptische Helena, Die (Hofmannsthal), 96–100

Aithra, 98–9

Ajax, 59

Alcestis: in Eschmann, 115–6; in Euripides, 103–5; interpretations compared, 116; legend of, 102–3; in Lernet-Holenia, 114–5; in Rilke, 113; in Wieland, 107–8; in Wilder, 108–12

Alceste (Wieland), 107–8

Alcestiad, The (Wilder), 101, 108–12, 172n

"Alcestis" (Rilke), 112–4

Alcestis: (Euripides), 103–5; (Hofmannsthal), 105–7; (Phrynicus), 172n; (Wieland), 173n

Alfieri, Vittorio, 16–7, 21

Alkestis: (Eschmann), 115–6; (Lernet-Holenia), 114–5; (Prechtl), 173n

Andromache, 8

Andromache (Euripides), 8–9

Anouilh, Jean, 125–6: *Antigone*, 139, 150, 156-61; *Médée*, 127–9

Antigone: Brecht on, 163–5; death wish of, 154, 159, 162–3; in Gide, 139; Hasenclever on, 163, 165–6; interpretations compared,

181